WEB ENGINEERING

Dr. Iqra Ameer

Toronto Academic Press

Web Engineering

Dr. Iqra Ameer

Toronto Academic Press
224 Shoreacres Road
Burlington, ON L7L 2H2
Canada
www.tap-books.com
Email: orders@arclereducation.com

ISBN: 978-1-77469-750-4

ABOUT THE AUTHOR

Iqra Ameer is an Assistant Professor at Penn State University, PA, USA. She received her Ph.D. in computer science with Distinction from the Instituto Politécnico Nacional, Mexico in 2022. During her Ph.D., she focused on multi-label emotion classification on code-mixed and monolingual text. She has extensive experience in tackling various challenges related to social media text, such as emotion classification, mental health illness, fake news, hate speech, toxic speech detection, and author profiling. Additionally, she has worked on suicide tendency prediction during her postdoc at Yale University and the University of Texas at Houston using clinical text. With her expertise in NLP, she has published several papers in top-tier conferences and journals.

Contents

List of Figures

List of Abbreviations

APM	Agile Project Management
ASP	Active Server Pages
ASP	Application Service Provider
CAD	Computer-aided Design
CDD	Constraint Directed Diagram
CFT	Call for Testing
CMS	Content Management Systems
CSC	Constraint Scenario Coverage
CSIS	Course Student Information System
DBMS	Database Management Systems
DCOM	Distributed Component Object Model
DEI	Data Envelopment Analysis
DOM	Distributed Object Middleware
EAI	Enterprise Application Integration
EDWs	Enterprise Data Warehouses
EJB	Enterprise Java Beans
FSM	Finite State Machines

GFSM	Guarded Finite State Machines
GFSMTT	Guarded Finite State Machines Test Tree
HCI	Human-Computer Interaction
IDEA	Interactive Data Extraction and Analysis
INWG	Internet Working Group
IT	Information Technology
JDBC	Java Database Connectivity
JSP	Java Server Pages
KPI	Key Performance Indicator
LC	Logic Component
MMS	Microsoft Media Server
MOM	Message-oriented Middleware
MPx	Emertxe Project Management
MTBF	Mean Time Between Failure
MVA	Mean Value Analysis
MVC	Model-View-Controller
NASA	National Aeronautics and Space Administration
NOAA	National Oceanic and Atmospheric Administration
ODBC	Open Database Connectivity
P2P	Peer-to-Peer
PNA	Progressive Networks Audio
PNM	Progressive Networks Metafile
QOS	Quality of Service
RAD	Rapid Application Development
ROI	Return on Investment
RPC	Remote Procedure Call
RTP	Real Time Protocol
SEI	Software Engineering Institute

SLA	Service Level Agreement
SOM	Service-Oriented Middleware
SPSS	Statistical Package for Social Sciences
TCO	Total Cost of Ownership
TCP	Transmission Control Protocol
TPM	Traditional Project Management
TTM	Time to Market
UAT	User Acceptance Testing
UCTM	Use Case Transition Models
UDP	User Datagram Protocol
UID	User Interaction Diagrams
UML	Unified Modeling Language
VSM	Virtual Shared Memory
WAA	Web Application Architectures
Was	Web Applications
WPA	Web Platform Architectures
WPMS	Web-based Project Management Systems
WRE	Web Requirement Engineering
xPM	Extreme Project Management

PREFACE

Today, the Web is essential to a wide range of intricate and sophisticated business applications. They have swiftly expanded in both their use and scope, having a huge impact on every aspect of our lives. Industries like manufacturing, tourism, hospitality, finance, education, and government are Web-enabled to improve and enhance their operations. E-commerce has rapidly grown and transcended international borders. As a result, we increasingly depend on a range of Web applications.

Now that so many of us rely on Web-based systems and services, they must be dependable and effective. Web developers require a robust methodology, a disciplined and repeatable process, better development tools, and a set of good rules in order to create these systems and applications. The online application still contributes to usability, quality, dependability, and other issues. It is necessary to provide some new techniques due to the numerous changes and improvements in web application characteristics.

Consequently, web engineering primarily concentrates on the procedures and strategies that are thought to be the fundamental building blocks of web applications. However, Web engineering isn't a clone of software engineering, despite the fact that both require programming and software development. It successfully creates, deploys, and keeps up high-quality Web systems and applications using scientific, technical, and management concepts. It aims to effectively manage the diversity and complexity of web applications, reduce risks, improve the quality and maintainability of Web sites, and bring order to the existing state of chaos in Web-based system development so as to prevent potential failures that could have detrimental effects.

This book attempts to solve the issue of an inadequate approach by providing an extensive and practical introduction to the field of web engineering. It introduces principles, strategies, methodologies, and tools for the methodical creation of Web applications by building on the lifespan of a Web application. It examines the distinction between Web applications and conventional software, the taxonomy of Web applications, the current stage of development, research problems, and the experience of creating a master's-level specialization.

The book provides a guide to the reader to understand the importance of the modeling need and hypertext modeling, along with challenges related to work. The reader is guided through the requirements of the Web engineering process for web applications and SWOT analysis of

RE for Web Apps. Readers are introduced to web application architecture, methods for web application integration testing, web in big data, data analytics, and issues in web application testing. Focus is also on WPMS, analytical approaches, and performance optimization procedures.

This book has been designed to suit the knowledge and pursuit of the researcher and scholars and to empower them with various aspects of web engineering so that they are updated with the information. I hope that the readers find the book explanatory and insightful and that scholars across various fields refer to this book.

– ***Author***

CHAPTER 1

AN INTRODUCTION TO WEB ENGINEERING

UNIT INTRODUCTION

This chapter will discuss the basic notion of web engineering, the motivation and need behind web engineering, the categories and characteristics of web applications, issues in web engineering, and how to improve web engineering practices.

Web engineering uses systematic, disciplined, and quantitative approaches to creating, managing, and maintaining Web-based systems. It is a proactive strategy as well as an expanding body of theoretical and empirical study in Web application development.

This chapter provides a general overview of web engineering by answering the following questions:

- Why is it necessary?
- What is its operational area?
- How does it assist with Web application development, and what should it do to improve it?
- How ought it to be incorporated into instruction and training?

The chapter examines the key distinctions between Web applications and conventional software, the taxonomy of Web applications, the current state of development, research challenges, and the experience of developing a master's-level specialization. The chapter concludes that Web Engineering, at this point, is a moving goal since web technologies are continually changing, opening the door for new kinds of applications, which may then call for changes in how they are created, deployed, and maintained.

Web engineering is the application of methodical, disciplined, and quantitative approaches to creating, managing, and upkeep Web-based applications. It is a reaction to the chaotic, early development of websites and applications, as well as the recognition of a gap between web developers and traditional software developers.

However, this list only represents a portion of the work done in the industry and the experiences of countless Web developers. According to a statement regarding software maintenance a few years ago, both excellent and bad practice is driving theory.

It provides a general understanding of web engineering. Although it inevitably includes contributions from scholars and practitioners worldwide, it is not an exhaustive evaluation of the work that has been published thus far.

A note on terminology: While discussing Web Engineering, the literature has used terms like Web sites, Web-based applications, Web-based systems, Web applications, and other variations of these. This chapter will use the term Web applications to represent all the variations.

In any case, websites (or Web apps) that provide information or assist users in carrying out tasks will be considered. Additionally, in order to save time, the phrase "Web development" will be used to refer to the creation, deployment, and maintenance of Web applications.

Learning Objectives

Following the completion of the chapter, the students should be able to understand the following:

- Understand web engineering;
- Identify the need for web engineering;
- Understand the categories of the web application;
- Give advice on web engineering motivation;
- Understand the characteristics of the web application;
- Educate about the differences in web engineering;
- Educate about how to improve web engineering.

Key Terms

- Framework
- Web

- Developers
- Expert
- Hypertext
- Application
- Content

1.1. WHAT IS WEB ENGINEERING?

Let's briefly answer the query in the section's headline: Web engineering suggests using an agile yet structured framework for building industry standard WebApp. Although it appears simple, you must understand two crucial terms in our response: agile and framework.

Remember

Web engineering is the application of systematic, disciplined, and quantifiable approaches to development, operation, and maintenance of web-based applications.

1.1.1. What is Meant by Agile?

Web engineers must be aware that modern business requires adaptation, business strategies, and rules change quickly, management demands near-instantaneous responsiveness (even when such demands are completely unreasonable), and stakeholders continually change their minds while also demanding quick delivery.

Customers care more about receiving a WebApp when they need it than they do about the amount of work required to produce a deliverable WebApp. A WebE team must prioritize agility in light of all of this. Ivar Jacobson offers a helpful explanation of the idea.

An agile team is quick to react to changing situations. Software development is very much about change. Changes in the software that is being developed, changes in the team members, changes brought on by new technology, and changes of all types could impact the product they develop or the project that produces the product.

Support for changes should be incorporated into every aspect of software development because it is the heart and soul of software's existence. An agile team understands that teams of people work together to produce software and that the project's success depends on the people's abilities to work well together and use their expertise.

According to Jacobson, the main force behind agility is the pervasiveness of change. Web engineers must be quick on their feet if they want to keep up with the rapid changes that Jacobson describes.

1.1.2. What is WebE Framework?

A framework identifies a small number of framework activities that are applicable to all WebApp projects, regardless of their size or complexity, and forms the basis for a full Web engineering process. A set of umbrella activities that are applicable to the full WebE process are also included in the framework. Each framework activity is filled with a set of Web engineering activities, which are a group of connected tasks that result in a work product (e.g., design is a WebE action). There are individual work tasks for each action that complete a portion of the work that the action implies. The following WebE tasks are a component of an overarching framework and are relevant to the great majority of WebApp projects:

- **Communication:** This involves close communication and collaboration with the client (and other stakeholders), as well as requirement collection and other associated tasks.
- **Planning:** This creates a progressive roadmap for the WebE work. It outlines the WebE actions that will take place, the technical tasks to be completed, the risks that are expected, the resources that will be needed, the work products to be created, and a work schedule.
- **Modeling:** This includes the creation of models to help the developer and the client better understand the requirements for WebApps and the design that will meet those requirements.
- **Construction:** It combines the creation of HTML, XML, Java, and other comparable code with the necessary testing to find problems in the code.
- **Deployment:** It presents a WebApp increment to the client, who then analyzes it and gives feedback in response to the evaluation.

Creating WebApps of any complexity and size is possible by utilizing these five general framework activities. Although the framework's specifics vary from case to situation, its functions always remain the same.

KEYWORD

WebApp is an application program that is stored on a remote server and delivered over the internet through a browser interface.

1.2. MOTIVATION BEHIND WEB ENGINEERING

The World Wide Web has a significant and enduring impact on our lives. The World Wide Web, or Web for short, has permeated almost every aspect of our everyday life, including the economy, industry, education, healthcare, public administration, and entertainment (Ginige & Murugesan, 2001b).

The primary cause of this omnipresence is the Web itself, which is known for its constant and universal accessibility as well as its uniform and comfortable access to information that is frequently dispersed and may be created by anybody as Web sites

(Berners-Lee, 1996; Murugesan et al., 1999). You most likely found this book by typing "web engineering" into a search engine. After using a portal to compare prices from several sellers, you might have utilized an online store to purchase the book.

TIPS

A Web application is a software system built on the World Wide Web Consortium's (W3C) technologies and standards that offers resources peculiar to the Web, like content and services, through a user interface, the Web browser.

The Web was once intended to be only an informational medium, but it is currently developing into an application media (Ginige & Murugesan, 2001a; Murugesan et al., 1999). Web apps today are fully-fledged, complicated software systems that offer customized, interactive, data-intensive services available through various devices.

They facilitate user interactions and typically store data in an underlying database (Kappel et al., 2002). The way that the Web is used, i.e., its technologies and standards are employed as a development platform and as a user platform at the same time, sets Web applications apart from traditional software applications.

A web application can therefore be defined as follows:

This term expressly includes both user interaction and technologies. We can conclude from this that technologies on their own, like Web services, are not Web apps, albeit they can be a component of one.

Further, this definition indicates that Web sites without software components, such as static HTML pages, are not Web apps either. Of course, more inclusive definitions are possible, such as ones incorporating websites and services (Baresi et al., 2000).

This book's conclusions can analogously address these situations. However, "limiting" the concept to Web applications that are software-intensive and interactive actually widens the scope of the issue because both the software and user interface parts of the Web must be investigated, which is one of the objectives of this book.

Despite the fundamental changes in the orientation of the Web from an informational to an application medium, the current situation of ad hoc development of Web applications reminds us of the software development practices of the 1960s, before it was realized that the development of applications required more than programming expertise (Murugesan, 2000; Pressman, 2000a; Retschitzegger & Schwinger, 2000).

Web application development is frequently viewed as a one-time event, frequently spontaneous, typically based on individual developers' skills, experiences, and development methods, limited to reuse in the sense of the "Copy & Paste paradigm," and ultimately characterized by insufficient documentation of design decisions.

Although this process may seem practical, such hasty development approaches frequently lead to serious quality issues, leading to serious problems with operation and maintenance. The applications created are frequently dependent on technology, prone to errors, and characterized by a lack of performance, stability, scalability, and user-friendliness, affecting acceptance (Fraternali, 1999).

The web's strong interlinking also increases the risk of issues transferring from one Web application to another. Complex factors have led to this circumstance (cf., e.g., Balasubramaniam et al., 2002; Ginige, 2000; Lowe, 1999; Murugesan, 2000; Murugesan & Ginige, 2005; Rosson et al., 2005):

- **Document-Centric Approach:** The building and connecting of websites, the inclusion of visuals, and the development of Web apps are all regarded to be authoring activities that are still frequently thought of as document-centric (Ginige et al., 1995). Although certain Web applications fall into this category (such as homepages, online newspapers, etc.), an authoring viewpoint is insufficient for creating software-intensive Web apps.
- **The Assumed Simplicity of Web Applications Development:** Simple web applications can be made without specialist knowledge with the wide accessibility of many tools, such as HTML editors and form generators (cf. Fraternali, 1999). Usually, visual design is prioritized over internal architecture and programming. This leads to contradictions and redundant information.

Know-how from relevant disciplines cannot be applied or is not used: A widespread misunderstanding is that the creation of Web apps can be compared to the creation of traditional programs and that, as a result, the methods of software engineering may be applied in the sense of a methodical, disciplined approach with sufficient quality control measures. This, however, appears inadequate in many cases due to the unique qualities of Web apps. Further, concepts and methods from relevant fields, such as hypertext or human-computer interaction (HCI), are frequently not used in a proper way (Deshpande et al., 1999). Due in part to the Web's relatively recent history, there are no development guidelines for high-quality Web apps.

KEYWORD

Human-computer interaction (HCI) is a multidisciplinary field of study focusing on the design of computer technology and, in particular, the interaction between humans (the users) and computers.

1.3. NEED FOR WEB ENGINEERING

The perspectives of developers and managers, their experiences in building applications made possible by new technologies, and the complexity of Web applications all influence how important (or unnecessary) web engineering is either perceived (or rejected).

White and Powell recognized the importance of engineering in the early stages of web development and underlined the necessity for Web Document Engineering and Web Site Engineering. Web engineering as a whole expressly acknowledges that high-quality Web development needs multidisciplinary effort and does not cleanly fit into any of the established disciplines.

1.3.1. Perceptions of Web Development

Web development is perceived at different levels:

- Web page construction;
- Web page design;
- Web site design;
- Web site construction;
- Web-based system;
- Web project planning and management.

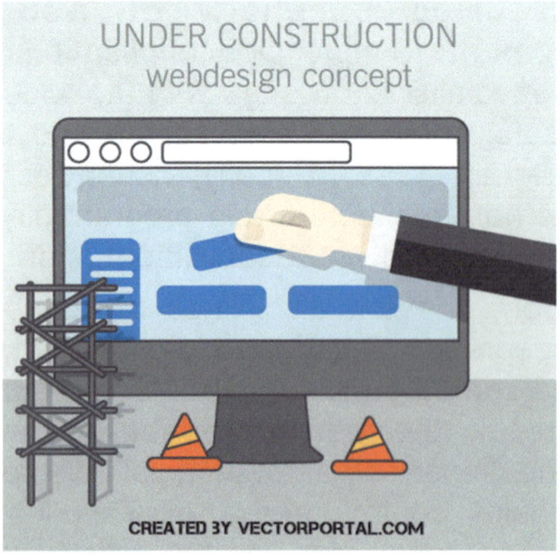

Figure 1.1. *Web page construction.*

Source: Image by Vector portal.

The web manifests itself through Web pages, the product of the simplest and most visible level, for someone who is relatively new to Web development, whether they are developers, users, or managers. Being based on a markup language (HTML) rather than a programming language makes it the easiest to comprehend and grasp (Figure 1.1).

As the managers and developers gain experience, the next level, web page design, becomes clear. If they have an IT background, they are aware that software developers need a variety of abilities that go beyond those found in computer science.

On the other hand, the importance of programming, databases, networks, and other IT areas may not become clear to non-IT managers and developers until much later. The page design, however, could not be seen as a difficulty given the abundance of packages that claim to lessen the load of page design.

These two levels equate to the user interface in terms of software engineering, which is typically seen as a subject of fine detail and more closely related to HCI. The next level of perception is related to web site design, or information architecture, as some people refer to it.

In this case, the hypertextual character of the Web is relevant since high-quality websites have clear navigational frameworks (i.e., structures that help its users achieve their goals). Traditional software engineering has not addressed this level at all, and it may require expertise outside of computer science.

KEYWORD

Web site is a collection of web pages and related content that is identified by a common domain name and published on at least one web server.

The fact that many organizations begin Web development at stage 3, when they have already decided they need to have a "Web presence," further compounds the perceptual challenges in this situation. As such, Web development may be primarily seen in terms of "publication" or "brand building/reinforcement," where lessons from software engineering are perceived as unimportant or are simply ignored.

Only when a Web site is developed and the knowledge that it is an information system, does it become evident how important additional stages are and what they entail. Therefore, the requirement for systematic, measurable, and repeatable development methods becomes clear.

Late realization of the value of web engineering could subsequently result in redesign and re-engineering of the current websites and applications, wasting time and resources. Software engineering is therefore applicable and essential at the application and project management levels, but it is insufficient for other activities.

Additionally, it is widely agreed upon, as will be detailed in further sections, that even in situations where software engineering is appropriate, newer and more advanced techniques of development, testing, and maintenance will need to be developed in order to address particular issues with Web development.

1.3.2. Web Developers' Experience, New Technologies, and Expert Consensus

Each workshop and conference described above are only a few places where the necessity for web engineering has been debated and discussed. Publications include journal articles, conferences, workshop proceedings, special issues of IEEE Multimedia, Cutter IT Journal, IEEE Software, and IEEE Internet Computing, and the edited book on Web Engineering.

KEYWORD

Software engineering is the branch of computer science that deals with the design, development, testing, and maintenance of software applications.

It is reasonable to conclude from these talks that the significance of and necessity for web engineering is now firmly established, thanks to an expert consensus on the key distinctions between the features of web applications and traditional software.

These distinctions are brought about by the new categories of (Web) applications rather than just the fact that many early Web developers lacked a background in software engineering. They have all discussed how the issues with application development during the time software engineering was initially presented and the current state of web development are comparable.

It is worth noting that this enumeration is based on the experiences of Web developers that the experts had consulted. Once the differences were identified, the question was raised as to whether current software engineering practices could address them successfully. The consensus was that software engineering was needed but not enough.

Two points are worth elaborating on. They both arise from the raison dieter of the Web, viz. communicating information globally. The first is the nature of information ("content is king") and its effect on developing a Web application. The second one is the nature of Web applications' end-users ("user satisfaction and threat of competition").

With regard to the information, information systems until now have dealt with largely transactional data in predominantly numerical form, with a bit of textual information, which can be more easily normalized, structured, sorted, and searched. Web-based information systems contain text and multimedia, which are difficult to structure, cannot be normalized, and are very hard to sort and search. Furthermore, they mix document orientation with database access through the hypertext metaphor.

As content, they are at this time 'integrated inextricably with procedural processing' (part of 'content is king,' above). Furthermore, they raise questions of information ownership and are mired in matters of legal, ethical, social, and legal issues.

Software developers did not deal with these issues in the past. Web developers must take them into account in creating Web applications. The implication is that if proper policies and procedures are not created, the work of Web developers may not achieve what the client wants.

Regarding the nature of the end-users, Web applications may address users anywhere in the world. Unlike the systems in use until now, Web-based ones are not always confined to specific user groups within an organization.

If Web applications were limited to intranets, the difficulties in understanding the users would be minimized. If they go beyond intranets, however, strategies and policies must be developed to better understand the potential, unknown, and perhaps unknowable users to establish the quality parameters of the applications to deliver quality systems, test sites, and applications and maintain security.

KEYWORD

Multimedia is the use of a computer to present and combine text, graphics, audio, and video with links and tools that let the user navigate, interact, and create; and multimedia is used to represent information in an interesting and interactive manner.

1.3.3. Characteristics and Complexity of Web Applications

Web applications vary widely: from small-scale, short-lived services to large-scale enterprise applications distributed across the Internet and corporate intranets. Over the years, Web applications have evolved and become more complex ñ they range from simple, read-only applications to fully fledged information systems. This complexity may be in terms of performance (number of hits per second), for example, the Slashdot site and the Olympics sites receiving hundreds of thousands of hits per minute, or in terms of the dynamic nature of information, the use of multimedia, or in other ways. They may provide vast, dynamic information in multiple media formats (graphics, images, and video) or may be relatively simple.

1.3.4. Multidisciplinary Nature of Web Development

Web applications handle information in its myriad forms (text, graphics, and video, audio). Information sciences, multimedia, hypermedia, and graphic design deal with structuring, processing, storing, and presenting this information.

HCI and requirements engineering are essential to understand users and their requirements. Network management, general computing, and simulation and modeling are required to deliver the information and desired functionality with an acceptable performance level. Software engineering, including new development methodologies, is essential for project and process management.

Since information is very often published for worldwide access, publishing paradigm, and legal, social, and ethical issues have to be taken on board. Consequently, good Web development must utilize relevant parts of all these disciplines and not be dominated by narrow viewpoints. Web Engineering is a response in recognition of the multidisciplinary nature of Web applications.

Interestingly, the ACM Computing Curricula 2001 formulates its first principle with a similar statement: "Computing... extends well beyond the boundaries of computer science." However, their recommendations cover the entire computing area, whereas Web Engineering concentrates on Web development (Figure 1.2).

Figure 1.2. *Website construction.*

Source: Image by Wikimedia Commons.

1.4. CATEGORIES OF WEB APPLICATIONS

Web applications have varying degrees of complexity. They may be purely informational or handle full-size/full-fledged 24/7 e-commerce applications. We must remember that there is a correlation between the chronology of development and complexity.

Workflow-based applications, for example, are transaction-based, i.e., the higher level of development requires the previous development of a less complex category. However, there may be exceptions to that rule in that some of the categories (e.g., the portal-oriented applications) are historically rather recent while having a lower degree of complexity.

Web presences of organizations that have been on the Web since their beginnings often have a development history. Of course, the development of a Web application can be started in any of these categories and later expanded to increasing degrees of complexity.

Newer categories are generally more complex, but this does not mean they can fully replace the older generation. Each of these categories has its own specific fields of application. Consequently, complex Web applications, in particular, can typically be assigned to several categories simultaneously.

Online shopping malls, for example, integrate different service providers and offer several search options, order status monitoring, and in some cases, even online auctions. Also, the different categories of Web applications cover many traditional fields of application, such as online banking, but at the same time, completely new fields of application are created, such as location-aware services.

Document centric Web sites are the precursor to Web applications. Web pages are stored on a Web server as ready-made, i.e., static, HTML documents, and sent to the Web client in response to a request. These Web pages are usually updated manually using respective tools.

Especially for Web sites requiring frequent changes or for sites with huge numbers of pages, this is a significant cost factor and often results in outdated information. Additionally, there is a danger of inconsistencies, as some content is frequently represented redundantly on several Web pages for easy access. The main benefits are the simplicity and stability of such Web sites and the

Did you Know?

Published contributions come from many sources, conference and workshop proceedings, journal articles, special issues of IEEE Multimedia, Cutter IT Journal, IEEE Software and IEEE Internet Computing, and the edited book on Web Engineering.

short response time, as the pages are already stored on the Web server. Static homepages, webcasts, and simple web presences for small businesses belong in this category.

With the introduction of the Common Gateway Interface and HTML forms, interactive Web applications emerged, offering the first simple form of interactivity by means of forms, radio buttons, and selection menus Web pages and links to other pages are generated dynamically according to user input. Examples of this category are virtual exhibitions, news sites, or timetable information.

KEYWORD

Online banking allows you to conduct financial transactions via the Internet.

- **Transactional Web Applications:** These were created to provide more interactivity, allowing the user to interact with the application in a read-only manner and perform updates on the underlying content. Considering a tourism information system, this would allow, for example, updating the content in a decentralized way or making it possible to book rooms.

The prerequisite for this is database systems that allow efficient and consistent handling of the increasing amount of content in Web applications and offer the possibility of structured queries. Online banking, online shopping, and booking systems belong to this category.

- **Workflow-based Web Applications:** These allow the handling of workflows within or between different companies, public authorities, and private users. A driving force for this is the availability of appropriate Web services to guarantee interoperability. The main challenges are the complexity of the services in question, the autonomy of the participating companies, and the necessity for the workflows to be robust and flexible.

Examples of this category are business-to-business solutions (B2B solutions) in e-commerce, e-government applications in the area of public administration, or Web-based support of patient workflows in the health sector.

Whereas workflow-based web applications require a certain structuring of the automated processes and operations, collaborative Web applications are employed especially for cooperation purposes in unstructured operations (groupware). There the need for communication between the cooperating users is particularly high.

- **Collaborative Web Applications:** These applications support shared information and workspaces in order to generate, edit, and manage shared information. They are also used to keep logs of many small entries and edits (as in Weblogs), to mediate meetings or make decisions as scheduling systems, or as e-learning platforms.

While originally, the Web was characterized by anonymity; there is an increasing trend towards a social Web, where people provide their identity to a (small) community of others with similar interests. Weblogs or collaborative filtering systems, for instance, serve the purpose of not only finding related objects of interest but also finding people with similar interests that belong to that category of applications.

- **Portal-Oriented Web Applications:** These provide a single point of access to separate, potentially heterogeneous sources of information and services. Makers of browsers, such as Microsoft and Netscape, search engines, such as Yahoo, online services such as AOL, media conglomerates, and other companies have become aware of the demand for this and now offer central hubs, so-called portals, as a point of access to the Web.

In addition to these general portals, there are various specialized portals such as business, marketplace, online shopping malls, and community portals. Business portals give employees and/or business partners focused access to different sources of information and services through an intranet or extranet.

Marketplace portals are divided into horizontal and vertical marketplaces. Horizontal marketplaces operate on the business-to-consumer market offering consumer goods directly to the general public and in business-to-business, selling their products to companies from other sectors. Vertical marketplaces consist of companies from a single sector, e.g., suppliers on one side and manufacturing companies on the other.

Community portals are directed at specific target groups, e.g., young people, and try to create customer loyalty through user interaction or to provide individual offers through appropriate user management (one-to-one marketing).

The increasingly important category of ubiquitous Web applications provides customized services anytime, anywhere, and for any device, thus facilitating ubiquitous access. An example of this would be displaying the menu of the day on the mobile devices of all users entering a restaurant between 11 am and 2 pm.

KEYWORD

Intranet is a computer network for sharing information, easier communication, collaboration tools, operational systems, and other computing services within an organization, usually to the exclusion of access by outsiders.

For this type of system, it is important to consider the limitations of mobile devices (bandwidth, screen size, memory, immaturity of software, etc.) and the context in which the Web application is currently being used. Based on this dynamic adjustment according to the users' situation (Kappel et al., 2002) can be made.

Currently existing web applications of this type usually offer a very limited form of ubiquity, only supporting one aspect – either personalization or location-aware services or multi-platform delivery (Kappel et al., 2003).

Current developments, however, especially the increasing convergence of the TIMES industry (telecommunications, information technology (IT), multimedia, education, and entertainment, security), will lead to a situation in the near future where ubiquitous applications will dominate the market. One of these developments is the Semantic Web.

TIPS

Web application development to cope with these two fundamental problems of the hypertext paradigm.

The Semantic Web aims to present information on the Web not merely for humans but also in a machine-readable form (Berners-Lee et al., 2001). This would facilitate knowledge management on the Web, particularly linking and reusing knowledge (content syndication) and locating new relevant knowledge, e.g., through recommender systems.

Through increased interoperation on the semantic level and the possibility of automating tasks (via software agents), we believe the Web will become even more ubiquitous and, therefore, relevant for everyday life.

1.5. CHARACTERISTICS OF WEB APPLICATIONS

Web applications differ from traditional, non-Web-based applications in a variety of features worth looking into. These are characteristics that traditional applications lack completely (e.g., non-linear navigation) on the one hand and characteristics that are of particular importance in Web applications on the other hand (e.g., frequency of updates).

Whether a certain characteristic is present and to what degree depends partly on the type of Web application: the development of transactional Web applications such as e-commerce systems requires greater focus on the content being up to date and consistent compared to pure information provision systems, e.g., virtual exhibitions.

These characteristics are the reason why many concepts, methods, techniques, and tools of traditional Software Engineering have to be adapted to the needs of Web Engineering or may even be totally inadequate. They along the three dimensions: "product," "usage," and "development," with their "evolution" as an encompassing dimension.

These dimensions are based on the ISO/IEC 9126-1 standard for evaluating software quality characteristics. By assigning the different characteristics of Web applications to these dimensions, we can also see their influence on the quality of applications and thus take the characteristics as a starting point for the definition of Web Engineering requirements.

In addition to product-related, usage-related, and development related characteristics, we have evolved as a fourth dimension governing the other three dimensions. Products must be adaptable, new contextual information should be considered during use, and development faces continually changing conditions, to name but a few examples.

Did you Know?

In 1999, the "web application" concept was introduced in the Java language in the Servlet Specification version 2.2.

1.5.1. Product-Related Characteristics

Product-related characteristics constitute the major building blocks of a Web application, consisting of content, the hypertextual structure (navigational structure), and presentation (the user interface). Following the object-oriented paradigm, each of these parts has not only a structural or static aspect, but also a behavioral or dynamic aspect.

1.5.2. Content

Generating content, making it available, integrating, and updating it is equally important as the development and provision of the actual software of a Web application. Web applications are used expressly because of the content they offer – true to the motto "Content is King."

Therefore, web application developers must act not only as programmers but also authors. Important aspects are the varying degree of structure of the content and the quality demands users make on the content.

- **Document-Centric Character and Multimodality:**

Depending on the structuring, content is provided as tables, text, graphics, animations, audio, or video. "Document character" in Web applications refers to the fact that content is provided, i.e., documents are generated that present information in an appropriate way for certain user groups (e.g., tourist information on a holiday region).

This implies, amongst others, special requirements for usability. Content is in part also generated and updated dynamically, e.g., the number of available rooms in a tourism information system. Furthermore, the Web serves as an infrastructure for the transmission of multimedia content, e.g., in video conferences or Real Audio applications.

KEYWORD

Mobile content is any type of web hypertext and information content and electronic media which is viewed or used on mobile phones, like text, sound, ringtones, graphics, flash, discount offers, mobile games, movies, and GPS navigation.

- **Quality Demands:** Depending on the application area, the content of a Web application is not only subject to differing update frequencies but also to different quality metrics regarding its being up to date, exact, consistent, and reliable. This requires not only the consideration of these quality demands in the requirements definition.

News sites, for instance, have a very high frequency of updates and face very high user demands regarding topicality. The Web, as a medium in its own right, alongside television, radio, and print media, offers great potential for addressing these demands better than traditional media, e.g., through personalization.

On the other hand, there is a line of argumentation saying that "smart," i.e., location aware, personalized applications, also require for new genres to be developed: the reason is that these new content-driven applications such as podcasting or mobile content are such a different medium that one cannot simply adapt existing content, but that rather new genres have to be developed in order to provide a high quality of user perception.

Particularly high quality is required for price and availability information in online shopping systems, as they form the basis of the business transaction. Incorrect prices can lead to a cancellation of the sale, and out-of-date information on availability can result in products in stock not being sold or in delivery problems because products listed as available are not in stock after all.

Regardless of where a Web application is used, content quality is a critical factor for its acceptance. The great challenge is being able to guarantee the quality of the data despite the large volume and high frequency of updates.

1.5.3. Hypertext

Web applications' specific characteristics are hypertextual documents' non-linear nature (Conklin, 1987). The hypertext paradigm as a basis for the structuring and presenting information was first mentioned by Vannevar Bush (1945). There are many different hypertext models (McCarty, 2003), and the Web itself defines a very simple model of its own (Figure 1.3).

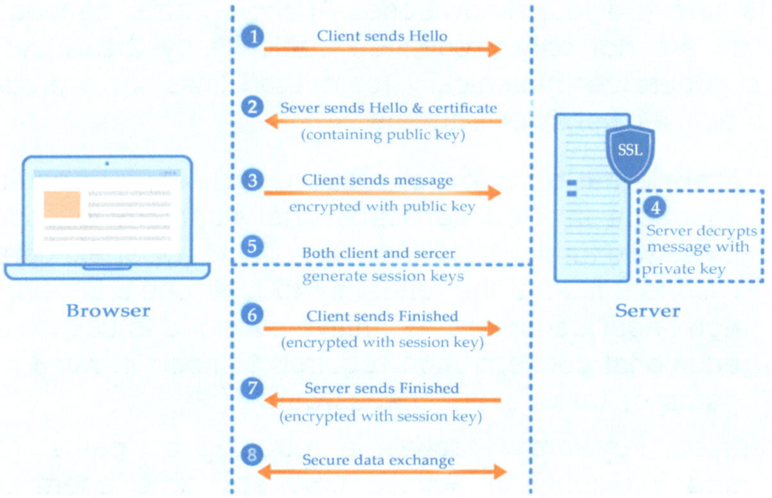

Figure 1.3. *What is HTTPS and why is it important for you?*

Source: Image by Seobility.

The basic elements of hypertext models are nodes, links, and anchors. A node is a self-contained, uniquely identifiable information unit. This might be an HTML document on the Web that can be reached via a URL (Uniform Resource Locator).

A link is a path from one node to another. These paths are always unidirectional on the Web, and their meaning is unclear. Possible meanings include "next node according to recommended reading order" or "diagram for mathematical formula."

An anchor is an area within the content of a node that is the source or destination of a link, e.g., a sequence of words in a text or a graphical object in a drawing. On the Web, anchors are only possible in HTML documents. The essential feature of the hypertext paradigm is the non-linearity of content production by the authors and of content reception by the users, together with the potential problems of disorientation and cognitive overload.

- **Non-Linearity:** Hypertexts imply stereotypes of relatively systematic reading, and in this, Web applications differ fundamentally from traditional software applications. We can distinguish among others between browsing, e.g., in online shopping applications, queries, e.g., in virtual exhibitions, and guided tours, e.g., in e-learning applications.

This individual reading style, adaptable to user needs and behavior, is ideally suited to human learning ability. Users may move freely through the information space, depending on their interests and previous knowledge. Anchors (and, consequently, also links) are not only predefined statically by the authors but are also generated dynamically (computed links) in a predefined reaction to user behavior patterns.

- **Disorientation and Cognitive Overload:** It is particularly important in Web application development to cope with these two fundamental problems of the hypertext paradigm. Disorientation is the tendency to lose one's bearings in a non-linear document. Cognitive overload is caused by the additional concentration required to keep in mind several paths or tasks simultaneously.

Remember

An agile team recognizes that software is developed by individuals working in teams and that the skills of these people, their ability to collaborate is at the core for the success of the project.

Sitemaps, keyword searches, a retracing of "paths" (history mode), and a display of access time and time spent on the site help users to keep their orientation within the application. Meaningful linking and intelligent link naming reduce cognitive overload (Conklin, 1987).

1.5.4. Presentation

Two special features of web applications at the presentation level, i.e., the user interface, are esthetics and self-explanation:

- **Aesthetics:** In contrast to traditional applications, the aesthetics of the presentation level of a Web application, the "look and feel" of the user interface, is a central factor, not least because of the highly competitive pressure on the Web.

The visual presentation of Web pages is subject to fashion trends and often determines success or failure, particularly for e-commerce applications (Pressman, 2005).

- **Self-Explanation:** Besides esthetics, it is essential that Web applications are self-explanatory, i.e., it should be possible to use a Web application without documentation.

The navigation system or interaction behavior must be consistent within the whole application so that users can quickly become familiar with the usage of the Web application.

1.6. ISSUES IN WEB ENGINEERING

An overview of issues in Web Engineering compared to traditional software engineering is discussed below:

- **Rush to Marked:** Web applications have a short time to-market (TTM) requirement. The average project time for Web Projects is under 3 months. The reason for this is partly the competitive environment on the Web. "Presence is everything." The technology for developing Web applications supports this desperate rush to market.

This is further intensified by the fact that application deployment is a matter of a few seconds and that the internet, the World Wide Web, and the availability of Web browsers created an international market with a breadth and scale of nearly inestimable potential.

- **Evolutionary Development:** Due to the desperate rush to market, we see a sense of extreme urgency in Web Engineering: obvious opportunities that someone else will grab unless the market is captured first and held against all newcomers that follow. The flexibility offered by the Internet environment makes it possible to deliver the desired functionality in chunks of successive releases.

Given that the market is willing to accept features in "installments," the cycle time for Web Applications is further compressed into short release cycles. This way of handling Web Development is called Web Gardening by some authors.

- **Requirement Management:** This issue is related to the previous one. The requirements for Web Applications are elicited during the development of the application. This is partly due to the changing market environment, which the customers have to respond to.

The technology that is used can also change. The result is that there is no formal requirement phase in many web development projects. Instead, prototypes are used to get feedback from both the customer and the user. Prototypes of web applications are also published to collect user feedback. As a result, thus, we need developers with an understanding of the applications' problem

KEYWORD

Navigation system is a computing system that aids in navigation.

domain. This understanding is needed when there are no formal requirement specifications.

- **Different Kinds of Market Environment:** The new market environment offers software products a new degree of flexibility in terms of requirements and quality factors. Web Applications are, in most cases, not mission-critical or life-critical.

Especially in the early stages of a product's introduction, organizations are willing to sacrifice some aspect of product quality for a shorter Time-to-Market. Requirements are negotiable from release to release in a market defined process.

- **Multi-Disciplinarily:** The development of Web Applications requires project teams with several skills. Activities involved in building Web Applications include content management, graphic design, and Human Computer Interaction.

TIPS

The average project time for Web Projects is less than 3 months.

Also, legal and ethical issues have to be considered. In addition to the technical activities we also find in traditional software engineering, this multidisciplinary result in some challenges for the development team.

An important issue is a communication between team members with diverse backgrounds, especially in light of the rush to market and the short development cycles.

- **The Nature of End-Users:** Web applications may address users worldwide. They are generally not confined to specific user groups within an organization. When Web Applications go beyond intranets, strategies, and policies must be developed to better understand the potentially unknown, and perhaps unknowable, users in order to establish the quality parameters of the applications so that they can deliver quality systems, test sites, and applications and maintain security.

1.7. HOW TO IMPROVE WEB ENGINEERING PRACTICES?

The WebSys project tries to find methods, guidelines, practices, and processes to help balance the conflicting requirements of short Time-to-market and reliability. The desperate rush to market comes at the expense of software with reduced quality. Some approaches which are investigated by the WebSys project are:

- Using standard architecture or product line architecture for Web Applications should help start new Web Applications projects with some proven components. This way, the quality of proven applications can be reused in new applications, and in the best case, TTM can be even shorter.

However, these components must fit into the ad hoc development practices used when developing new Web Applications.

- Another topic investigated by the WebSys project is the use of patterns for Web Development.
- The use of Model-Driven Development can also speed up the development time of Web Applications while addressing quality issues. There exist some Web Application development environments that let the developer specify Web Applications by using UML models.
- Another way to improve Web Engineering Practices would be to have a process model for Web Engineering where the evolving process can be controlled. Such a process should also support the special requirements of a Web Development process.

The WebSys project is working with a Web Development process that uses several Trade-off techniques to speed up decision making and enhance team members' communication.

KEYWORD

Model-driven development is a format to write and implement software quickly, effectively and at minimum cost.

SUMMARY

- **Web Engineering and the Need:** This chapter summarizes web engineering. What is meant by agile? And WebE Framework has also been explained in this chapter.

  The need for web engineering has also been briefly discussed in this chapter, and the steps are perceptions of web applications, web developers' experience, new technologies and expert consensus, characteristics and complexity of web applications, and multidisciplinary web development.
- **Categories and Characteristics of Web Application:** The end of the chapter summarizes the categories of the web application. They may be purely informational or handle full-size/full-fledged 24/7 e-commerce applications. They also discussed the characteristics of web applications – in addition to product-related, usage-related, and development related characteristics.

REVIEW QUESTIONS

1. What do you mean by web engineering?
2. What is meant by agile?
3. Explain the need for web engineering.
4. Discuss the categories of web applications.
5. Explain the characteristics of web applications.
6. Explain the difference in web engineering.
7. How to improve web engineering?

MULTIPLE CHOICE QUESTIONS

1. A ___________ team must emphasize agility.

a. WebE

b. Host

c. Client

d. Router

2. What Number of generic framework activities can be used during the development of Web Apps?

a. 1

b. 3

c. 4

d. 5

3. How many ways can web development be perceived at different levels?

a. 5

b. 4

c. 6

d. 3

4. In content which motto is used?

a. Content is King

b. Content is Queen

c. Content doesn't matter

d. None

5. HTTP stands for

a. Hypertest Technology Protocol

b. Hypertext Technology Protocol

c. Hypertext Transfer Protocol

d. Hypertest Transfer Protocol

Answers to Multiple Choice Questions

1. (a) 2. (d) 3. (c) 4. (a) 5. (c)

REFERENCES

1. Deshpande, Y., et al., (2002). *Web Engineering*, https://arxiv.org/. Rinton Press. Available at: https://arxiv.org/ftp/cs/papers/0306/0306108.pdf (accessed on 04 March 2023).
2. Ginige, A., & Murugesan, S., (2001). Web engineering: An introduction. *IEEE Multimedia, 8*(1), 14–18. Available at: https://doi.org/10.1109/93.923949.
3. Ginige, A., (2016). Web engineering: An introduction. *IEEE Multimedia*. academia.edu. Available at: https://www.academia.edu/18521108/Web_engineering_an_introduction (accessed on 04 March 2023).
4. Pressman, R. S., & Lowe, D., (2009). *Web Engineering a Practitioner's Approach*. www.skylineuniversity.ac.ae. McGraw-Hill. Available at: https://www.skylineuniversity.

ac.ae/pdf/software-engineering/Software%20Engineering%20a%20practioners%20approach%20by%20Rober%20S.%20Press%20-.pdf (accessed on 04 March 2023).

5. *Web Software Engineering,* (n.d.). www.egyankosh.ac.in. IGNOU. Available at: https://egyankosh.ac.in/bitstream/123456789/10291/3/Unit-1.pdf (accessed on 04 March 2023).

CHAPTER 2

REQUIREMENTS ENGINEERING FOR WEB APPLICATIONS

UNIT INTRODUCTION

The previous chapter discusses the basics of web engineering, its need, and how it can aid in web applications. Also, the categories, as well as the characteristics of web applications, have been explained. So, now the current chapter will be more about the concept of requirement engineering, as it can be assumed as the backbone of web engineering. The chapter will discuss the fundamentals of requirement engineering, its principles, specifics, etc.

The creation of Web applications is heavily dependent on requirements. However, requirements are frequently not expressed correctly and may be confusing, vague, or wrong. Low user acceptance, unsuccessful planning, or insufficient software designs are typical effects of inadequate requirements.

In system development, identifying, describing, validating, and managing requirements are all topics covered by RE. Numerous RE techniques and tools are accessible today. However, practitioners frequently don't use these methods, and RE work is frequently done in an ad-hoc manner, especially in Web engineering. Although the complexity of modern Web applications necessitates a more systematic approach, the RE process's maturity is frequently insufficient.

The challenge of defining requirements is not new. Software Requirements: Are They Really a Problem? Was the title of their 1976 article? Bell and Thayer stress that requirements must be identified during an engineering effort because they do not arise automatically (Bell & Thayer, 1976).

Early in the 1980s, Boehm researched the cost of requirements faults and discovered that early detection and rectification of defects save up to 200 times the cost of late removal of undetected defects (Boehm, 1981). According to Brooks' article No Silver Bullet: Essence and Accidents of Software Engineering, gathering and refining requirements iteratively is one of a software engineer's most crucial tasks for a client (Brooks, 1987).

There is broad agreement regarding the significance of requirements for effective system development, and over time, a variety of standards, methods, models, description languages, and tools have appeared. However, the software business continues to face significant challenges with regard to requirements:

- According to a survey in 1995 involving 340 businesses in Austria, more than two-thirds of these businesses viewed the creation of a requirement document as a significant issue with their development process. Additionally, more than half of the companies considered requirements management to be a serious issue (European Software Institute, 1995).
- According to a Standish Group study of more than 8,000 projects, 30% of all projects failed before they were finished, and 70% of the remaining projects fell short of consumers' expectations. In more than half of the cases, the observed issues were closely related to the requirements, including poor user participation, incomplete or volatile requirements, unrealistic expectations, imprecise objectives, and unrealistic schedules (The Standish Group, 1994).
- According to research conducted by the Cutter Consortium on the creation of Web applications, it was found that only 16% of the systems fully met the contractors' demands, while 53% of the systems that were really deployed lacked the necessary capabilities (Cutter Consortium, 2000).

Although there is universal agreement that RE is important and valuable for achieving schedule, budget, and quality goals, there are frequently issues with the actual adaption and usage of current processes, elicitation methodologies, notations, and tools. This is particularly true for creating Web applications because there is still little expertise compared to other areas, and requirements are frequently acquired, recorded, and managed unsystematically.

Learning Objectives

Following the completion of the chapter, the students should be able to understand the following:

- Understand the fundamentals of web engineering; where do its requirements come from?
- Understand web engineering skills;

- Understand the pedagogical foundation;
- Understand the design of the Pedagogical Model;
- Understand the Requirements of Engineering principles;
- Educate about the SWOT analysis of RE for web apps;
- Understand the RE specifics in web engineering.

Key Terms

- Fundamentals
- Engineering
- Pedagogical
- Foundation
- Negotiating
- Stakeholders
- Validation

2.1. FUNDAMENTALS OF REQUIREMENT ENGINEERING

2.1.1. Where Do Requirements Come From?

The unique objectives and expectations of stakeholders initiate the process of gathering requirements. Stakeholders are people or organizations that can directly or indirectly affect the needs for system development (Kotonya & Sommerville, 1998). Customers, users, and developers are significant stakeholders. Typical Web application stakeholders include content creators, domain experts, usability experts, or marketing specialists. As seen by a few examples, the objectives and expectations of stakeholders are frequently quite diverse:

KEYWORD

User interface is the point of human-computer interaction and communication in a device.

- The web application shall be available online by September 1, 2006 (customer constraint).
- The web application shall support a minimum of 2,500 concurrent users (quality objective of the customer).
- J2EE shall be used as a development platform (technology expectation of developer).
- All customer information must be transmitted securely (quality objective of the user).
- The user interface must accommodate various customer group layouts (quality goal of the customer).
- A random user must be able to locate a desired product in less than three minutes (usability objective of the customer).
- The user will be able to choose an icon to show the items currently in their shopping cart at any time (capability objective of the user).

The main function of project management is identifying and involving stakeholders whose participation is essential to project success. Understanding and frequently resolving divergent goals, expectations, backgrounds, and agendas is a difficult task.

Conflicts could arise, for instance, between a desired set of capabilities and the available money, between the intended set of capabilities, the project timetable, and the required quality, or perhaps between a desired development technology and the abilities and expertise of the developers. Early recognition and resolution of these inconsistencies and conflicts are critical and contribute significantly to risk management. To facilitate this effort, negotiation strategies have been proposed (Grunbacher & Seyff,

2005). A prerequisite for success in this approach is creating a shared vision among the stakeholders.

Stakeholder objectives are frequently expressed informally and serve as the basis for determining more specific needs. A requirement details a quality that must be met or a service that a system must offer. According to IEEE 610.12, a requirement is a condition or capability that a system or system component must meet to comply with a contract, standard, specification, or other formally imposed documents. It can also be a documented representation of a condition or capability, as in (1) or (2).

TIPS

Important quality characteristics include accuracy, objectivity, credibility, relevance, actuality, completeness, or clarity (Strong et al., 1997).

Functional requirements, non-functional requirements, and constraints are typical categories for requirements (Robertson & Robertson, 1999). Functional requirements specify the capabilities and services of a system, while non-functional requirements (such as "How secure?" and "How usable?") outline desirable quality levels.

Constraints are equally significant because they are unavoidable conditions that affect a project. Examples of constraints include the level of expertise of the development team, the available funds, the deadline for delivery, or the pre-existing computer infrastructure in the deployment environment.

2.1.2. Requirements Engineering Activities

The term "RE" refers to the management of requirements throughout the development process, including their elicitation, documentation, verification, and validation.

- **Requirements Elicitation and Negotiation:** According to research, "requirements are not readily available to be gathered by asking the correct questions" (Nuseibeh & Easterbrook, 2000). Instead, requirements are the outcome of a process of learning and forming consensus (Boehm et al., 2001; Lowe & Eklund, 2002). Communication between the parties involved in this process is crucial since only their combined experience can result in solutions that are acceptable to both parties.

Various techniques and collaborative tools are available to facilitate communication and knowledge exchange in RE. Examples include Techniques like creativity, scenario-based procedures, multi-criteria decision making, facilitation techniques, interviews, or document analysis (Nuseibeh & Easterbrook, 2000).

- **Requirements Documentation:** If all stakeholders reach an agreement, their agreements must be clarified and stated in a requirements document with the level of formality and complexity required for a project context. Based on the project risks that have been identified, as well as the knowledge and abilities of the anticipated readers, the appropriate level of formality and detail should be chosen. In Web Engineering, informal descriptions like user stories and semi-formal descriptions like use cases are especially important.
- **Requirements Verification and Validation:** It is necessary to validate and verify requirements. "Did we specify the proper items?" and "Did we specify things correctly?" Various traditional techniques for achieving this goal include reviews, inspections, and prototypes (Halling et al., 2003). The Internet's accessibility in Web engineering enables new ways for users to directly participate in requirements validation, for as through the online gathering of user feedback (Deshpande et al., 2002).
- **Requirements Management:** Requirements are frequently altered rather than being stable. An important aspect of Web projects is the constant changes in needs and restrictions. New requirements and updates to existing requirements are both supported by requirements management techniques and technologies.

KEYWORD

Agreement is the state or act of agreeing, meaning coming to a mutually approved arrangement.

They assist in evaluating the effects of changes by controlling dependencies between requirements and between requirements and other development artifacts (traceability). In order to facilitate this work, technologies are often utilized due to the challenges of requirements management for even moderately complicated systems.

2.2. WEB ENGINEERING SKILLS

Given the state of web engineering, the ability of web engineers to master the development process is the most important determinant of the success of web engineering projects.

Thus, identifying the abilities that one anticipates Web engineers to have been a crucial step in teaching web engineering (Reichgelt et al., 2004). According to Seffah & Grogono (2002), three categories of abilities are necessary for any software engineer.

- Any student entering the profession of web engineering must possess the first set of prerequisite abilities. Early skill development is essential since Web engineering education depends on them.
- The second group is focused on particular Web engineering skills. It enables the execution of significant Web engineering development process activities.
- The third category, referred to as general abilities, includes project planning, teamwork, communication, reading, and other skills. These abilities are necessary for Web engineers in a professional setting.

2.3. REQUIREMENTS ENGINEERING PRINCIPLES

In this section, we are going to know the RE principles and their details. These nine principles are discussed in subsections.

KEYWORD

Project planning is a discipline addressing how to complete a project in a certain timeframe, usually with defined stages and designated resources.

2.3.1. Value Orientation

Writing requirements isn't a goal for RE. The act of writing requirements based on assumptions has no value, neither for the users nor for your business. The requirements outcomes need to add value for the users. Remember, users use products to do their job better. The requirements should add value to the outcome and the benefit of using your product in end-users' life.

2.3.2. Stakeholders

Using RE helps you do your best to satisfy the stakeholders' needs and desires. When we speak about developing a digital product, many product people think they should just deliver a product based on end-user needs.

Well… that won't work. When you want to develop a digital product that brings a delightful experience with itself, you need to consider all the people and organizations that make an impact on the product or are impacted by that product. According to the IREB's glossary, we call these organizations and people the stakeholders.

To consider stakeholders very well, designing different personas and categorizing stakeholders are the critical activities that you like a product people need to do. To do so, focus on categorizing stakeholders in these categories:

- Critical: Most important ones, if you don't consider engaging them, you are going to develop a useless product, and they can make the product fail.
- Major: These are the ones that have an important role in product success. They greatly impact a product's success, but the product won't fail by not considering them.
- Minor: Not considering these stakeholders will not have an impact or a minor impact on product success.

Remember

A pedagogical model is a conceptual construct that can be used by teachers as a framework for instruction using a specific learning theory (Nunes & McPherson, 2003).

2.3.3. Shared Understanding

All the stakeholders need to have a shared understanding of the problems and their related requirements. It is very important to know the shared understanding's enablers, such as shared culture and values, informed mutual trust, previous successful collaboration, domain-specific standards, etc.

Also, to make this happen, product people have to know the obstacles and find the solutions for them. Obstacles like geographical distance, outsourcing, and regulatory constraints need to consider carefully during the RE.

2.3.4. Context

Product people should be aware that products cannot be understood in isolation. One of the most critical principles of RE is context. The context is a part of the product's environment is somehow relevant and helps understand the product and its requirements. Determining the right product context and its elements helps you find the right requirements to solve in the future with the product.

2.3.5. Problem, Requirements, Solution

People use products to do their jobs better, faster, easier, and with a joyful experience. Whenever they are not satisfied when doing their jobs, there is a problem. Every problem needs a solution that can solve it and improves the situation and experience. Finally, requirements related to the problem must be elicited to make a solution useful, valuable, and worthwhile. So, as you see, these three are completely and closely related together.

2.3.6. Validation

Validation is not just for the increments or the mature product. It starts with the requirements. In order to develop a digital product that satisfies stakeholders' needs and desires, you need to validate the elicited requirements.

According to IREB, validation is the process of confirming that the document requirements match the stakeholders' needs and desires. Or, in other words, confirming whether the right requirements have been specified.

2.3.7. Evolution

Digital products exist in a world that contains EXTREME change. Desires, needs, processes, jobs, behaviors, and capabilities change continuously. So, the digital product must embrace the change to show its value and improve its capability to deliver an experience satisfying the users.

Remember that you, as a product, should manage the evolution; otherwise, it manages you and guides the product through failure.

TIPS

The web apps as have short time to market (TTM) requirement and are rushed to marked.

2.3.8. Innovation

Innovation is a key principle of the RE. It reminds product people that they are not the stakeholders' voice recorders. They should be innovation aware. They are going beyond whatever the stakeholders tell them to make them happy and excited. In order to make disruptive innovations happen, product people need to explore possible disruptive ways of doing their jobs that make them achieve their goals with a better experience.

2.3.9. Systematic and Disciplined Work

Well, the last one is this... systematic and disciplined work. Systematic and disciplined work goes hand in hand with processes. To do your best with the requirements, you need a suitable process to systematically elicit, document, validate, and manage the requirements. This process helps you develop a product with a certain, appropriate level of quality that satisfies the stakeholders.

2.4. SWOT ANALYSIS OF RE FOR WEB APPS

SWOT is an acronym for strengths, weaknesses, opportunities, and threats. A SWOT analysis (SWOT matrix) is a structured planning method used to evaluate strengths, weaknesses, opportunities, and threats involved in a project (Figure 2.1).

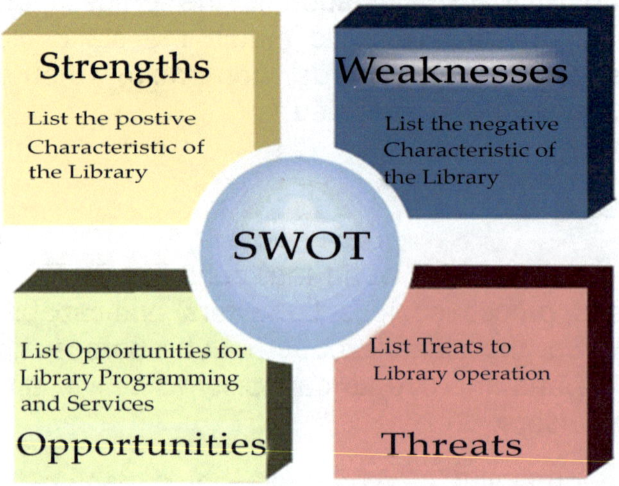

Figure 2.1. SWOT analysis.

Source: Image by Flickr.

It is an analytical technique that is commonly used as part of strategic planning as a foundation for evaluating the internal potential and limitations and the probable/likely opportunities and threats from the external environment. It views all positive and negative factors inside and outside the area/field that affect the growth/scope.

The analytical technique of SWOT presented here addresses and urges researchers to make significant improvements to understand and work in the web requirement engineering (WRE) domain. The subsections expound on the details.

2.4.1. Strengths

- **Effective Classification of Diverse Users:** The problem of large numbers of stakeholders in the case of web applications is solved by classifying them into different groups for the purpose of requirement elicitation and specification.

As web applications may be accessed by a large number of diverse users distributed over the world, thus it is necessary to recognize each type of user community so that each may be benefited from the purpose of the application, and WRE techniques fulfill this necessity.

- **Various Types of Elicitation Approaches:** Various requirement elicitation techniques are available for web applications, from which anyone could be selected for the required purpose. They may be classified into different categories based on their approach.

These may include a navigational approach, conceptual approach, interface-based approach, prototype-based approach, etc. Navigational approaches focus on possible patterns of web page access by different categories of already classified users.

It helps reset the navigational pattern of links in the best suited way, thus satisfying each user community's needs. Prototype based approaches reduce time by performing requirement engineering along with the design phase, thus handling and managing requirements at the same time.

KEYWORD

User community is a digital space designed for a software product's users.

It is an iterative process in which requirements are recognized and defined based on the prototype developed. Interface based approaches, along with traditional types of requirements, also focus on user interface requirements. In web applications, the user interface plays a very vital role that cannot be neglected.

- **Powerful Specifications Techniques:** User interaction diagrams (UID) are very strong tools for aiding web requirement gathering as well as the specification process. They serve as a communication bridge between the user and the designer. Use-case diagrams and UIDs are combined to express requirements, which can also be used to validate requirements.

Also use of sketches, mock ups, and, more importantly, the use of natural languages in the specification of requirements in web application development makes the validation task effective for both users and analysts and the requirement gathering tasks easy for users and customers.

- **Emphasize on Non-Functional Requirements:** Regarding web applications, non-functional requirements include a fast data exchange rate between client and server, high data and network security, user satisfaction, data quality, and representation, etc.

That is why; WRE techniques give equal weightage to non-functional requirements. In the validation phase of requirements, mainly non-functional requirements are validated.

- **Content Driven:** Web applications generally manage content and not just data, and many web applications are document-centric versus data-centric. Content has its own value when talking about web applications. That's why requirements are considered for producing, gathering, storing, and modifying content.
- **Social Feedback and Prioritization of Requirements:** Social feedback means inviting feedback from web users about any issue. This mechanism is very helpful in gathering and analyzing requirements. Social feedbacks are of three types: comments, rating, and voting. Comments are open arguments and discussions about requirements to help improve it, Rating is about judging quality on a scale (generally a 5-point scale), and voting shows acceptance by the user.

KEYWORD

Social feedback is the acknowledgment of other people's content on social media through likes,

These social feedback mechanisms might be very helpful for authors of requirements as they give some hints about where a requirement needs to be improved or more precisely defined. Also, these can furthermore provide a valuable starting point for the prioritization of requirements.

2.4.2. Weaknesses

- **Difficult to Design Architecture:** In order to make the requirement specification process easier and more effective, from the customer's perspective, the task of software developers to design the architecture becomes difficult.

In web applications, techniques used for requirement specification like sketching, mockups, use of natural language, and others no doubt make the requirement specification process much easier but make designing a little bit complicated for designers.

- **Difficulty in Convincing Method:** A methodology is primarily created by accumulating the experience of failures or overruns encountered in previous projects. It is difficult to convince that methods or models can be applied in another environment.
- **Compressed Development Schedules:** The web apps need to be deployed quickly and require design choices to

be made accurately within a very compressed development life cycle as the time pressure is heavy.

Nearly every project faces shortened product release cycles and escalating pressures for timely delivery, but the Web redefines the notion of accelerated development and deployment. Web apps have a short time to market (TTM) requirement and are Rushed to market. The average project time for Web Projects is under 3 months.

- **Small Team with Diverse Background:** Web Apps are often developed by a small team of people with diverse backgrounds, skills, and knowledge. Moreover, it has to accommodate non-developers, especially management, when designing or recommending architecture and policies.

As compared to a team of software developers, their perception of the web and the quality of web based systems is considerably different, causing confusion and misguided priorities.

KEYWORD

Web-based system provides access to a software system using a computer and internet connection.

2.4.3. Opportunities

- **General Elicitation Technique:** All approaches for requirement elicitation for web applications can be combined to develop a single powerful requirement elicitation technique covering all advantages of each distinct approach.

Thus, a generalized approach can be developed, powerful enough to beat any specific technique in terms of their individual advantages of using them.

- **Requirement Traceability:** Currently, requirement traceability is supported by only some of the available requirement elicitation techniques for a web application like NDT, and OOWS. This is an indivisible feature of any WRE process, as this is the only way to handle newly inserted requirements during application development at some later time.
- **Early Threat Detection and Avoidance:** Current environment enacts the problem once it is detected rather than enacting after detection, thus just mitigating the effect of the problem. Avoidance of problems should be a more adaptable technique.

The key is detecting threats before they fail and proactively switching to an alternative configuration involving different commitments to avoid failure. For this purpose, risk assessment is carried out, and risk is associated with each requirement specified.

But when dealing with web application development, it seems more difficult to find the criticality of the risk due to a huge diversity in types of users using the application. Thus, there is a scope in the field of risk assessment and attachment to the requirement.

2.4.4. Threats

KEYWORD

Communication is usually defined as the transmission of information.

- **Lack of Effective Communication:** The Web is full of diversities, and in such an environment, setting up a communication link between all stakeholders and then executing it effectively is a difficult task and any little deviation from the planned activity for communication may born possibilities for unclear and redundant requirement extraction.

For example, we have a very powerful technique, social feedback and prioritization of requirements, for gathering requirements from diverse users, but what if the users themselves do not participate in feedback? This may create severe problems in the task of WRE, which in turn will severely affect the further development of the web application.

- **Requirement Traceability Problem:** The inability to trace the human sources of actual requirements and their related information is identified as the crux of the requirements traceability problem. As the application development process continues, some new requirements could be introduced, and then in order to check that these newly introduced requirements do not conflict with present requirements, communication is needed to be established with human sources of the requirements.

To solve this problem, link with individual sources rather than with groups or community, should be established, but in the case of web applications this task may be a threatening one cause of the diversity and unavailability of the application users.

- **Effective Classification of Users (Strength may Turn into Threat if Done Incautiously):** While creating an application for web users, it is mandatory to classify users into proper groups so that an actual and complete set of requirements can be gathered. This task must be implemented cautiously, assigning weightage to the requirement gathering process and requirements gathered for each user group properly; otherwise, the strength may become a threat.

- **Rapidly Evolving Implementation Environment, Encompassing Various Hardware Platforms:** Web Apps are built in a constantly changing environment, i.e., the requirements are unstable and continuously evolving. So, web app development is not a one-time event; rather, it is a process with an iterative lifecycle to cope with various supporting hardware, software, and networks.
- **Social, Legal, Ethical Issues:** Web Applications serve global audiences and norms, and laws may be different where Web Apps are defined as opposed to where they are utilized. Further, Web Apps, as discussed, are content driven, so there may also be information ownership issues. Thus, cultural or regional considerations, privacy, moral, and legal obligations and requirements pose a serious threat.

KEYWORD

Hardware refers to the computer's tangible components or delivery systems that store and run the written instructions provided by the software.

2.5. RE SPECIFICS IN WEB ENGINEERING

How does RE for Web Engineering differ from RE for conventional software systems? On the surface, the differences seem to be negligible, as argued by researchers in the field: "While there are many differences between Web development and software development, there are also similarities between them. These include requirements elicitation." However, differences become apparent if we take a closer look at some specifics.

- **Multidisciplinary:** The development of Web applications requires the participation of experts from different disciplines. Examples include multimedia experts, content authors, software architects, usability experts, database specialists, and domain experts.

The heterogeneity and multidisciplinary of stakeholders make it challenging to achieve consensus when defining requirements. This problem is compounded as people from different disciplines have their own languages and jargon that need to be reconciled.

- **Unavailability of Stakeholders:** Many stakeholders, such as potential Web users, are still unknown during RE activities. Project management needs to find suitable representatives that can provide realistic requirements. For example, there is often a wide spectrum of possible users in Web projects, and finding a reasonable set of representatives is hard.

- **Volatility of Requirements and Constraints:** Requirements and constraints such as properties of deployment platforms or communication protocols are often easier to define for conventional software systems than for Web applications. Web applications and their environments are highly dynamic, and requirements and constraints are typically harder to stabilize.

KEYWORD

Open-source software is computer software that is released under a license in which the copyright holder grants users the rights to use, study, change, and distribute the software and its source code to anyone and for any purpose.

Frequent examples of changes are technological innovations, such as the introduction of new development platforms and standards or new devices for end users.

- **Unpredictable Operational Environment:** The operational environment of a Web application is also highly dynamic and hard to predict. Developers find it hard or impossible to control important factors that are decisive for the user perceived quality of a Web application.

For example, changing bandwidths affect the response time of mobile applications but are outside the sphere of the development team.

- **Impact of Legacy Systems:** The development of Web applications is characterized by the integration of existing software components such as commercial off-the-shelf products or open source software. In particular, Web developers frequently face the challenge of integrating legacy systems, for example, when making existing IT systems of a company accessible through the Web.

Developers are often asked to use existing components for economic reasons. The components that need to be integrated strongly influence the requirements and architectural style of the future system.

Under such circumstances, a waterfall approach to derive the system architecture from requirements will not succeed, as existing components, services, and infrastructure define the range of possibilities and limitations for the developers. This means that Web developers must be aware of the system architecture and architectural constraints when identifying and defining requirements.

- **Significance of Quality Aspects:** Quality aspects are decisive for the success of Web applications. Examples include the performance of a Web application, security as in e-commerce, availability, or usability. Despite the significance of quality aspects, developers have to deal with the problem that an exact specification of quality requirements is often hard or even futile before the actual system is built.

For example, the response time of a Web application depends on many factors that are outside the control of the development team. A feasible approach for defining quality requirements is to specify criteria for the acceptance test indicating whether or not a requirement has been met.

- **Quality of the User Interface:** The quality of the user interface is another success-critical aspect of Web application. When developing Web applications, developers need to be aware of the IKIWISI (I Know It When I See It) phenomenon: users will not be able to understand and evaluate a Web application by just looking at abstract models and specifications; rather, they need to experiment with it.

It is thus absolutely essential to complement the definition and description of requirements by adding prototypes of important application scenarios.

- **Quality of Content:** Many traditional RE methods neglect Web content, though it is an extremely important aspect of Web applications. In addition to software technology issues, developers have to consider the content, particularly its creation, and maintenance.

In the context of RE, it is particularly critical to define the required quality of content. Important quality characteristics include accuracy, objectivity, credibility, relevance, actuality, completeness, or clarity (Strong et al., 1997).

Content management systems (CMS) gain importance and allow the representation of content concisely and consistently by separating content from layout, and offering content editing tools.

- **Developer Inexperience:** Many of the underlying technologies in Web applications are still fairly new. Inexperience with these technologies' development tools, standards, languages, etc., can lead to wrong estimates when assessing the feasibility and cost of implementing requirements.
- **Firm Delivery Dates:** Many Web projects are design-to-

Did you Know?

Constructivism is grounded in several philosophical traditions with three orientations: individual constructivism, social constructivism, and radical constructivism.

schedule projects, where all activities and decisions have to meet a fixed final project deadline. The negotiation and prioritization of requirements are particularly crucial under such circumstances.

SUMMARY

- **Fundamentals of Web Applications:** This chapter summarizes about the fundamentals of web applications. Where do the requirements of web application come from and Requirements engineering activities? The different Web Engineering Skills have also been explained in this chapter.

  The designing of the pedagogical model and the pedagogical foundation has also been briefly discussed in this chapter. The steps are managing the learning process, setting the learning context, stating the challenges and learning goals, Assessing the student's prerequisite knowledge and skill level, negotiating authentic tasks, constructing web based applications, reflecting and self-evaluating, conducting a formative assessment, presenting, and communicating the results.
- **Requirements Engineering Principles:** The different requirements of engineering principles have been explained under this heading. They are: value orientation, stakeholders, shared understanding, context, problems requirements solution, validation, evolution, innovation, and systematic and disciplined work.
- **SWOT Analysis:** The end of the chapter summarizes about the SWOT analysis of RE for Web apps. The strengths, weaknesses, opportunities, and threats are explained. The chapter summarizes with the Re specifics in Web Engineering.

REVIEW QUESTIONS

1. Where do the requirements for web engineering come from?
2. What are Web Engineering Skills?
3. What are the different steps in designing a Pedagogical Model?
4. What are the requirements of engineering principles?
5. What do you understand by the term Stakeholders?
6. Explain the difference between Evolution and innovation?
7. What is the acronym for SWOT?
8. What do you understand by threats in Web Engineering?

MULTIPLE CHOICE QUESTIONS

1. A ___________ is a special computer that serves webpages.

a. Server
b. Host
c. Client

d. Router

2. **Which analysis is a part of the Analysis model of the web engineering process framework?**
   a. Content analysis
   b. Interaction analysis
   c. Functional analysis
   d. All of the above
3. **What category of web-based system would you assign to electronic shopping?**
   a. Informational
   b. Interactive
   c. Transaction-oriented
   d. Workflow-oriented
4. **Which process model should be used in virtually all situations of web engineering?**
   a. Incremental model
   b. Waterfall model
   c. Spiral model
   d .None
5. **Which web app attribute is defined by the statement: "The quality and esthetic nature of content remains an important determinant of the quality of a WebApp"?**
   a. Availability
   b. Data driven
   c. Content sensitive
   d. Continuous evolution

Answers to Multiple Choice Questions

1. (a) 2. (d) 3. (c) 4. (a) 5. (c)

REFERENCES

1. Aurum, A., & Wohlin, C., (2005). *Engineering and Managing Software Requirements*. www.repository.dinus.ac.id. Springer. Available at: https://repository.dinus.ac.id/docs/ajar/%5BAyb%C3%BCke_Aurum_(Editor),_Claes_Wohlin_(Editor)%5D_En(BookFi.org)_.pdf (accessed on 04 March 2023).

2. Hadjerrouit, S., (2005). Designing a Pedagogical Model for web engineering education: An evolutionary perspective. www.jite.org. *Journal of Information Technology Education*. Available at: https://jite.org/documents/Vol4/v4p115-140Hadj50.pdf (accessed on 04 March 2023).
3. Kappel, G., et al., (2006). *Web Engineering the Discipline of Systematic Development of Web Applications, PDF Book Preview*. John Wiley & Sons. Available at: https://www.free-ebooks.net/academic-science/Web-Engineering/pdf/preview (accessed on 04 March 2023).
4. Kappel, G., et al., (n.d). *The Discipline of Systematic Development of Web Applications*. 123dok.com. John Wiley and Sons. Available at: https://123dok.com/document/zx98m2wz-the-discipline-of-systematic-development-of-web-applications.html (accessed on 04 March 2023).
5. Toma, I., & Komazec, S., (2013). *Requirements Engineering for Web Applications*. www.sti-innsbruck.at. Available at: https://www.sti-innsbruck.at/sites/default/files/courses/WE-02-Requirements.pdf (accessed on 04 March 2023).
6. Ziapour, A., (2022). *Fundamental Principles of Requirements Engineering: The key to Product Success*. www.ProductSchool.com. Product School. Available at: https://productschool.com/blog/product-management-2/fundamental-principles-requirements-engineering-product/ (accessed on 04 March 2023).

CHAPTER 3

MODELING WEB APPLICATIONS

UNIT INTRODUCTION

The first generation of Web applications for e-commerce, content management, and publication concentrated on enabling users to carry out basic tasks like searches, data uploads, and browsing through vast amounts of material organized in hypertexts.

More recently, the Web has gained popularity as a platform for B2B apps, which aim to integrate both intra- and inter-organizational business activities in addition to content navigation. Web-based B2B applications display much more sophisticated interaction patterns than traditional Web applications because they are created to support a well-defined process, which consists of activities and the limitations on how they can be carried out while also providing services to various user roles whose collaborative work is coordinated.

Due to organizational limitations, design opportunities, or the presence of legacy systems that can be reused, they may be spread among various processing nodes. B2B Web applications require innovative study, definition, and implementation approaches because they are more complicated than process-based systems or pure data-centric Web applications.

Workflow models and design techniques give complicated B2B applications notations capable of expressing process specifications, capturing activity execution limitations, and capturing unique process aspects like pro-activity, exception management, and mistakes compensation. These models are supported by a class of specialized products called Workflow Management Systems, which allow for the definition of process schemes, their administration, and a guarantee of performance, scalability, and distribution. However, many applications do not make investing in specialized process administration software worthwhile. Therefore, it is becoming more common to use general-purpose design support environments to aid in the creation of these applications. These environments start with the specification of process modeling abstractions, which are typically supported by graphical representations, and end with their encoding in programming languages like C++ or Java.

Web application design has primarily focused on data-centric applications, like Web Information Systems, emphasizing design methodologies capable of expressing a wide variety of navigation patterns, on the relationships between content modeling and hypertext modeling, and special classes of applications like multi-channel, collaborative, and adaptive Web applications. By utilizing details about the user and the user's current execution context, these technologies currently offer dynamic Web page production and personalization. These approaches do not, however, provide thorough design procedures that integrate cutting-edge Web application design techniques with traditional business process analysis techniques.

Additionally, the pull-based HTTP protocol that supports Web applications lacks easy mechanisms for interactions started by the server; this inherent challenge must be overcome by employing approaches and techniques that include server-initiated operations and asynchrony. Designers can express process requirements regarding Web interactions carried out by human agents using notions from process modeling. The usage of Web Services enables designers to model process distribution requirements resulting from organizational constraints, design opportunities, or existing legacy systems.

Using their preferred BPMN editor, developers can model their business processes, manually convert the models into a set of WebML specifications in accordance with the desired distribution architecture and coordination policy, and then use Web Ratio to specify the hypertexts and automatically generate the code that implements such applications to be installed at the various nodes of the chosen architecture.

Since "explicit" design styles can be automated, we plan to build a tool that can convert a BPMN diagram into a collection of WebML diagrams that reflect the skeletons of the Web apps that support the process.

Learning Objectives

Following the completion of the chapter, the students should be able to understand the following:

- Understand the modeling of web-based applications;
- Understand the challenges in modeling web applications;
- Understand the model driven design of web applications;

- Understand the integration of business processes and web application development;
- Understand the content modeling;
- Understand hypertext modeling.

Key Terms

- Modeling
- Integrating
- Hypertext
- Requirements
- Applications
- Business

3.1. MODELING WEB-BASED APPLICATIONS

Handling the software's dynamic nature is a crucial component of conducting web application analysis—and may be the most challenging part of the process. Uncertainty in program behavior, modifications to application needs, the rapid evolution of web technology itself, and other factors cause the dynamic elements.

The dynamic nature of web software poses difficulties for analysis, testing, and maintenance, in addition to another significant issue. Is it required to modify every component connected to an application when one component changes?

We proceed by creating an analytical model that uses a regular expression notation to represent the components of dynamically generated web pages. The analysis model can be used to build tests, support implementation, and comprehend how changes to one component will affect the rest of the application.

TIPS

Modeling the content in the sense of pure data modeling is normally sufficient for static Web applications.

3.1.1. Analysis Model

The main sources of complexity in web software analysis are the dynamic aspects, such as dynamically created client components, dynamic client-server interaction, and ongoing changes in the system context and web technologies. We begin with the essential component of web applications, the interactions, to adequately illustrate its dynamic nature. Then, extra features are induced into the model.

Even though interactions among clients and servers are unpredictable, there is a common theme that can be used. Web applications usually work in the following way. First, a client often collects information from servers in the form of HTML files, then submits requests to servers, and finally anticipates responses in the form of HTML files.

Of course, not all interactions take place through HTML pages, but most web applications are currently processed this way. The assumption is that clients and servers communicate via HTML pages. In the future, we hope to pursue implementations of this model's ideas in other forms of interactions, such as XML-based applications.

To simplify processing, we assume that each online application uses a portal, or a single start page S, an HTML file that starts the application's navigation. If there are many portal pages (S1, S2, ..., Sk), it is presumed that a start page specific to each portal page can be built. Clients and servers communicate with one another, starting with the start of page S through requests and HTML files. Most of the content in early web applications was kept on servers as static HTML pages, images, and data files.

As web technology developed, elements from various files and program statements were combined to create dynamic HTML files. We first illustrate the fundamental elements that may be constructed to simulate the interactions of web apps. Then we define a set of operations that can be utilized to create new compound elements.

A static HTML file or a portion of a server application that prints HTML is called an "atomic segment." An atomic section has the "all-or-nothing" property, which states that either the full section is delivered to clients or none of it is. A static HTML section with content variables or a constant HTML section both fall under the category of "atomic sections." An HTML page receives data from a program variable known as a content variable but not structure.

3.1.2. Web Applications

A web application is frequently set up in a three-tiered manner. The middle tier includes the application server that communicates with the database and other web objects, as well as the web server that implements CGI, PHP, Java servlets, or active server pages (ASP). Finally, the database and DBMS server comprise the third tier (Figure 3.1).

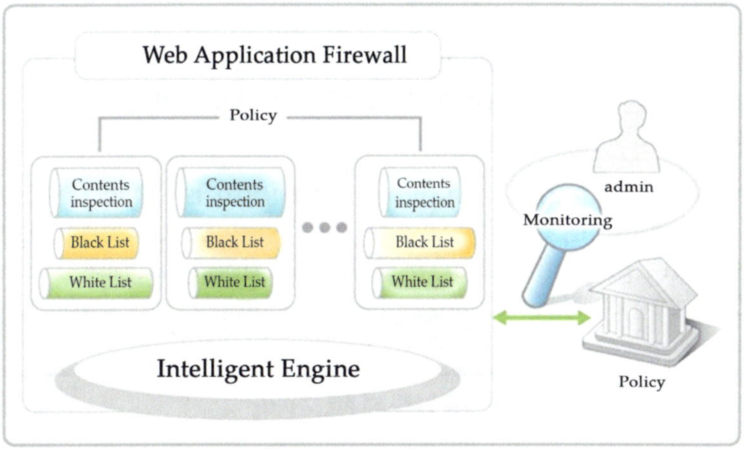

Figure 3.1. *3rd generation WAF.*

Source: Image by Wikimedia Commons.

Different types of information, including text, graphics, and forms, are included in the web pages that web applications create. These web pages can be either static or dynamic. Only HTML and client-side executable code, such as JavaScript, can be found on static pages, which are stored on a web server and provided by the server.

Dynamic pages are generated as a result of numerous scripts and server components being executed, dynamic pages. The application server serves these sites, which mix HTML source code with executable code.

According to some researchers, a website is merely a collection of connected web pages gathered on a server or in a server folder. These pages are static and don't use dynamic features; therefore, the application servers don't need to process them.

KEYWORD

JavaScript is a programming language that is one of the core technologies of the World Wide Web, alongside HTML and CSS.

Whether these qualities are static, dynamic, or interactive, all methods that offer models to capture various aspects of the structure (navigation), behavior, and content of web applications are of interest to us.

The presentation level, which specifies how data will be provided to consumers, is another level that could be considered. Attributes like color and font, as well as cascading style sheets, are all issues related to this level.

3.1.3. Web Services

A standardized way of integrating web-based apps is through the use of distinct service communication interfaces that other online applications may access. They are generally utilized as a way for companies to communicate with clients and with one another while avoiding disclosing specific information about each other's IT systems.

The most common communication form is XML, independent of any particular operating system or computer language. Web services don't give the user a GUI and don't require the user to use a browser or HTML.

3.2. MODELING REQUIREMENTS

Use cases are the preferred modeling technique for functional requirements, not least because they can be represented graphically.

The overall functionality of a Web application is modeled as a set of use cases, which describe the Web application requirements from the actors' (people and other systems) perspectives.

Additionally, use cases can be supplemented by UML activity diagrams to describe the functional requirements in more detail. One peculiarity of Web application requirements is navigation functionality, which allows users to navigate through the hypertext and find nodes.

Suggests separating the functional from the navigational use cases, creating two distinct models. Another approach (UWE), selected herein, is to create one single use case model, which uses the UML navigation stereotype to denote the difference between functional and hypertext-specific use cases.

All Web applications have at least one human user, most often anonymous. In our example of an online conference paper reviewing system (referred to as "the reviewing system" in the following), four actors can be identified: users of the reviewing system, authors submitting papers to the conference, members of the program committee (reviewers) reviewing papers submitted, and the chair of the program committee (PC chair).

Use cases should be described in detail. We can describe each use case in textual form or by use of a behavior diagram, e.g., an activity diagram. Activity diagrams are mainly used when use cases are based on more complex application logic. Such a use case, for example, might be implemented as a Web service.

TIPS

Data modeling is a well- established discipline and may be addressed through well-known models like Entity-Relationship and UML.

3.3. MODEL-DRIVEN DESIGN OF WEB APPLICATIONS

The first generation of conceptual models for the web (Schwabe & Rossi, 1998; Fernandez et al., 1998; Mecca et al., 1999; Ceri et al., 1999, 2000, 2002; Gomez et al., 2001) essentially considered Web applications as a variant of traditional hypermedia applications, with the particularity that the published contents are extracted from a database, and user interaction with the application takes place via the medium of the Internet (Figure 3.2).

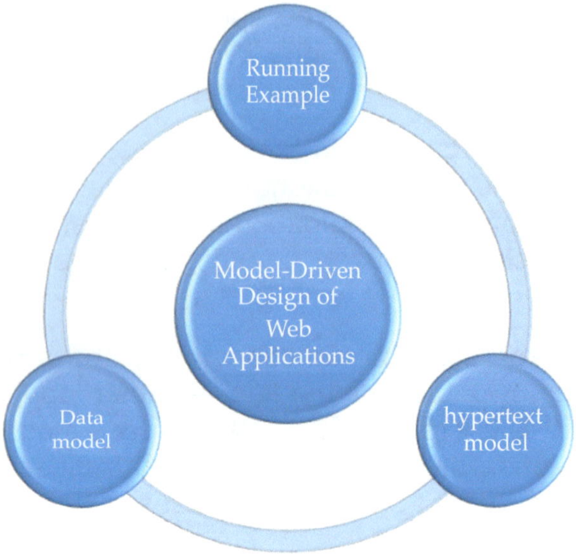

Figure 3.2. *Model driven design of web application.*

Therefore, these modeling approaches have focused on capturing the structure of the application contents, e.g., as a set of object classes or entities connected by associations or relationships, and the navigation primitives, represented by such concepts as pages, content nodes, and links. One such model is WebML, described by Ceri et al. (2002). WebML allows specifying a Web site on top of existing data sources. A conceptual model consists of a data schema describing application data and of one or more hypertexts (called site views) expressing the Web interface used to publish and manipulate such data.

3.3.1. Running Example

In the sequel, we will use a running example to illustrate the hypertext and process modeling primitives at the base of the proposed approach. The running case consists of a loan brokering Web application.

Three classes of users enact the overall process for loan requests management: bank clients, who may apply for loans, receive responses from the bank, and choose among the approved requests the actual loan options to purchase; bank employees, who must perform in parallel a financial and a job status check on each submitted loan request; and managers, who perform a preliminary validation of each request at the beginning of the process, and ultimately approve or reject the request, based on the outcome of financial and job status checks performed by the bank employees.

3.3.2. Data Model

The WebML data model is the standard Entity-Relationship model widely used in data design. We use a simplified Entity-Relationship notation, in which entities are represented as rectangles (including the entity name and the list of attributes) and are connected by binary relationships, represented as straight lines labeled with the relationship name.

Relationship specification includes the minimum and maximum cardinality of participation of each entity in the relationship, denoted by the cardinality values (0, 1, or N) attached to the relationship line. The schema also comprises entity User, describing the users of the Web applications, and entity Group, denoting groups users with similar characteristics: each user may belong to multiple groups (denoted by a relationship between entity User and Group), and one group is the default one (denoted by relationship Default).

TIPS

BPMN and UML behavioral diagrams (use cases and activity diagrams) have similarities in both their purposes and notations.

The Loan Proposal relationship specifies that a Loan may be associated with various Loan Proposals and that each Loan Proposal refers to just one Loan. Relationships are also characterized by relationship roles (usually omitted for lack of space), representing the two directions in which the relationship can be navigated.

3.3.3. Hypertext Model

The main ingredients of the WebML hypertext model are site views, areas, pages, units, operations, links, and session/application variables. A site view is a graph of pages, possibly grouped into areas, allowing users of a given group to perform their specific activities (e.g., users browse the information while managers update it). Consider, for instance, a simple scenario: users browse a Home Page, from where they can navigate to a page showing an index of loan products. After choosing one loan, users are led to a page with the loan details and the list of proposals for the chosen loan.

The Home Page contains only some static content, which is not modeled. A link from this page leads to the Loans page, containing an index of all loans, graphically represented using an index unit labeled Loans Index.

When the user selects a loan from the index, he is taken to the chosen loan page, showing the loan details. On this page, a data unit, labeled Loan Details, displays the attributes of the loan (e.g., the company, the total amount, and the rate) and is linked to another index unit, labeled the proposals index, which displays all the plan options of the loan.

- **Contextual Links:** The content of units displayed on a page is often related to that of other units; this connection is achieved by contextual links, carrying data between the related units. It transports the ID of the loan chosen in the index unit and displayed in the data unit.

The data carried by a contextual link is not always shown in a WebML diagram explicitly because, in many cases, it can be inferred from the context. For example, a link exiting from an index unit always carries the identifier of the chosen object; a link going out from a data unit carries the identifier of the object displayed by the unit, etc.

KEYWORD

WebML is a visual notation and a methodology for designing complex data-intensive Web applications.

Thus, links exiting from the Loans Index and Loan Details units in the example implicitly carry as context a Loan ID.

- **Transport Links:** WebML distinguishes between normal links (denoted by solid arrows) and transport links (denoted by dashed arrows). Normal links enable navigation and are rendered as hypertext anchors or form buttons; they can be contextual or not.

This particular link is not contextual since it carries no information and simply enables a change of page. In contrast, transport links are always contextual.

For example, the link from the Loan Details data unit to the Proposals Index unit is a transport link: when the user enters the Chosen Loan page, the Loan Details unit is displayed and, at the same time, the content of the Proposals Index unit is computed and displayed without user's intervention. No navigable anchor is rendered for transport links.

- **Selectors:** The content of a unit may depend on selectors, which are (possibly parametric) predicates. The Loan ID transported from the Loan Details to the Proposals Index unit is used to select the options associated with the loan by the relationship role loan to the proposal.

This selection is expressed by the selector condition below the unit's entity, which ensures that only the loan proposal instances connected to the chosen Loan via the Loan Proposal relationship are retrieved to build the index. In general, conjunctive logical conditions can be used, where each conjunct is a predicate over an entity's attribute or relationship role.

- **Operations:** WebML allows specifying update operations on the data underlying the Web application. Basic update operations are the creation, modification, and deletion of instances of an entity or the creation and deletion of instances of a relationship.

Other operations may include sending an e-mail or, as we will see, invoking Web services. Unlike units, operations do not display data; therefore, they are not included on a page.

The chosen loan page contains an entry unit representing a form collecting user data. When the user submits the data by clicking on the outgoing link of the entry unit, the entered data is used to create a new loan proposal instance in the data repository.

KEYWORD

Data repository is a data library or data archive.

A create operation represents data creation. After the creation, the new instance is connected to the currently selected Loan by means of a connecting unit. Connect units create a new instance of a relationship. WebML includes several other units and operations (such as Modify unit for data updates and the Disconnect unit for relationship removal), a customizable mechanism for dealing with run-time failures, and is extensible by the user, who can add their custom units.

3.4. INTEGRATING BUSINESS PROCESSES AND WEB APPLICATION DEVELOPMENT

This section discusses how to extend conceptual modeling from data-centric Web applications to data- and process-centric ones. We start by presenting development lifecycle extensions to incorporate process modeling into the design of Web applications, even if existing data-centric Web design methods do possess enough expressive power to capture the requirements of business process modeling, describing process-aware Web applications solely in terms of data and hypertext modeling concepts leads to poor separation of concerns and hard-to-maintain specifications and implementations.

3.4.1. Development Lifecycle of Process-Centric Web Applications

The phases of Web application development centered on processes and data. In line with the classic Boehm's Spiral model and with modern methods for Web and software engineering, the development phases must be applied iteratively and incrementally, in which the various tasks are repeated and refined until results meet the business requirements. At each iteration, the current version of the system is tested and evaluated and then extended or modified.

Requirements specification is the activity in which the application analyst collects and formalizes the essential information about the application domain and expected functions. This aspect does not significantly differ from requirement collection for traditional applications.

KEYWORD

Data design is the first design activity, which results in less complex, modular and efficient program structure.

Data design is the phase in which the data expert organizes the main information objects identified during requirements specification into a comprehensive and coherent conceptual data model. Data modeling is a well-established discipline and may be addressed through well-known models like Entity-Relationship and UML.

Data modeling for Web applications does have a special flavor due to the role that information objects play in such a context, but we do not address this issue here. Hypertext design is the activity that transforms the functional requirements identified during requirements specification into one or more site views embodying the needed information delivery and data manipulation services.

Hypertext design operates at the conceptual level, possibly exploiting high level models, which let the hypertext architect specify how content elements are published within pages and how hypertext elements are connected by links to form a navigable structure.

Of the entire lifecycle, hypertext design is the phase that most benefits from a conceptual approach because its application results in a more consistent and qualitative design. Additional tools, like design patterns and best practices, further facilitate the task of the hypertext designer.

With respect to a purely data-centric Web application, the Conceptual Design phase of process-intensive applications includes the Process design task, focusing on the high-level schematization of the processes underlying the application. The Process distribution task addresses the allocation of sub-processes to different peers and therefore occurs only when several Web servers are involved in the process enactment. Process design and distribution influence data and hypertext design, which should consider process requirements. However, depending on the designer's sensibility, process design can be postponed with respect to data design if data assume a more central role in the application. The other phases are outside the scope of this chapter, and we briefly cite them for completeness.

Architecture design defines the hardware, network, and software components that make up the physical architecture by establishing the mix of these elements that best meets the application requirements; implementation is the activity of producing the software modules and database schemas necessary to transform the data and hypertext design into an application running on the selected architecture; finally, testing and evaluation is the activity of verifying the conformance of the implemented application to the functional and non-functional requirements.

Remember

The use of process modeling concepts enables designers to specify process requirements in terms of interactions on the Web, enacted by human agents.

Maintenance and evolution comprise all the modifications effected after the application has been deployed in the production environment.

However, a reference development lifecycle based on a formal methodology and appropriate high-level modeling concepts is useful to better incorporate change management into the production mainstream. It greatly reduces the risk of breaking the software engineering process due to the occurrence of changes. This is fundamental in the Web environment, where applications are subject to fast evolution.

3.4.2. Process Modeling With BPMN

Many high-level notations have been proposed to express process structure. We adopt the business process management notation [W+04], which comprises the following concepts:

- **Processes:** High-level descriptions of the work to be globally performed.
- **Actors:** The users performing the work.
- **Activities:** The units of works composing a process, typically performed by a single actor.
- **Constraints:** The logical precedence among activities. BPMN constraints assume a variety of forms:
  a. **Sequence:** A sequence is a combination of two (or more) activities that can be executed only in sequential order (i.e., one after another). One activity must finish before the next one can start.

b. **AND-Split/AND-Join:** At the split point, the execution flow is spawned in two (or more) parallel branches, thus enabling mandatory parallel execution of two (or more) activities. All the branches must be executed.

Parallel execution is not considered in a strict temporal sense but only requires the parallel activation of all the branches, which can be executed either simultaneously or with some delay.

In particular, parallel branches that the same actor must execute are likely to be executed in sequential order; however, the executor can choose any order.At the joining point, two (or more) parallel execution branches merge into a single flow after all branches are completed. This means that AND join is a blocking gateway, in the sense that all the branches must complete for the process to advance.

KEYWORD

Parallel execution is a means to test multiple applications or multiple components of an application at the same time.

c. **OR-Split/OR-Join:** At the split point, a single control thread decides which branches to take among several alternative branches. Notice that an arbitrary (non-empty) subset of the available branches can be executed in any order.

At the joining point, two or more alternative branches converge to a unique thread of control in a non-blocking way, in the sense that the first branch that completes can trigger the prosecution of the process.

d. **XOR-Split/XOR-Join:** A single control thread decides which branch to take among several alternative branches. Only one alternative can be triggered in this case, and all the other branches are disabled. The XOR-join operator behaves in a similar way to the OR-join.

e. **Iterations:** The repeated execution of one or more activities.

f. **Pre- and Post-Conditions:** Entry and exit criteria to/from a particular activity, respectively.

1. **Cases:** The specific executions of an individual process instance.
2. **Activity Instances:** The specific executions of activity within a case.

Processes can be pictorially represented with the Business Process Management Notation (White, 2004a), which is adopted by the BPML standard (2006) issued by the Business Process Management Initiative.

The BPMN notation visually represents all the process concepts defined above and provides further constructs, such as more powerful conditional gateways, event and exception management, a free combination of split/join points, and other minor extensions.

BPMN and UML behavioral diagrams (use cases and activity diagrams) have similarities in both their purposes and notations. However, UML is focused on object behavior and primarily devoted to supporting the software development process, from architecture design to implementation, and is conceived for use by technically skilled developers. Conversely, BPMN is more centered on processes and is more suited to business analysts.

Events occur during the process execution. They are categorized by their type, distinguishing messages, time events, and rule firings; appropriate symbols can be put into the circle representing the event to denote the type. Gateways are process flow control elements; typical gateways include the decision, splitting, merging, and synchronization points.

Various logical behaviors are allowed for the gateways. Activities are the basic tasks of the process and can express various behaviors. The flow of activities inside the process is described by means of arrows, representing either the actual execution flow, the flow of exchanged messages, or the flow of data objects between activities.

Grouping operators permit the clustering of activities into pools. One pool contains all activities enacted by a given process participant. In our context, we will consider a participant to be a peer involved in the distribution process. Within a pool, we use BPMN lanes to distinguish user types interacting with a specific peer.

The process occurs within a single pool consisting of three parallel lanes (represented as horizontal rectangular areas), one per type of user. The process starts with a loan request issued by an applicant, which is submitted for preliminary validation to a manager. The manager may either reject it (if the application is not valid), which terminates the process or assign it in parallel to two distinct employees for checking. After both checks are complete, the manager returns the application and makes the final decision. Finally, the customer chooses among the options provided for his request.

KEYWORD

Business analyst is a person who processes, interprets and documents business processes, products, services and software through analysis of data.

3.4.3. WebML Primitives for Conditional Navigation

Enforcing process constraints via hypertexts requires conditional navigation. This is needed, for instance, to implement XOR and AND gateways and to evaluate logical conditions before/after activity execution. The behavior of the If and Switch unit is similar to the equivalent programming language constructs, but they govern the navigation in a WebML hypertext.

If the unit has one or more incoming links and one associated logical expression, only one of the two outgoing links is activated, depending on whether the logical expression evaluates to true or false. Notice that there is no guard condition on the outgoing links, but a single Boolean condition is associated with the unit; therefore, only one of the two outgoing links can be enabled.

KEYWORD

Content modeling is the process of creating a logical taxonomy structure for the content you create and distribute online.

The Switch unit has an associated expression, and each outgoing link has a guard condition testing the equality of the expression to a given value; only one of the outgoing links whose guard condition is true is followed as the result of the navigation, possibly selected non-deterministically.

3.5. CONTENT MODELING

The information provided by a Web application is one of the most important factors for the success of that application, not least due to the origins of the Web as an information medium. Modeling the content in the sense of pure data modeling is normally sufficient for static Web applications. Complex Web applications additionally require the modeling of behavioral aspects.

This means that content modeling includes creating the problem domain model, consisting of static and dynamic aspects, as known from traditional Software Engineering. In addition, the following web application characteristics have to be considered:

- **Document-Centric Character and Multimedia:** It is necessary to consider all kinds of different media formats when modeling the content, including the structures the information is based on.
- **Integration of Existing Data and Software:** Many Web applications build on existing data repositories and software components that were not originally created for

Web applications. Content modeling has to satisfy two potentially contradicting objectives, i.e., it should cover the content requirements of the Web application to the best possible extent, and it should include existing data structures and software components.

3.5.1. Objectives

Content modeling is aimed at transferring the information and functional requirements determined by requirements engineering to a model. This effort will not consider the hypertext character of a Web application and its presentation requirements.

Content modeling produces a model that comprises both the structural aspects of the content, e.g., in the form of a class diagram, and, depending on the type of Web application, the behavioral aspects, e.g., in the form of state and interaction diagrams.

Did you Know?

The web server that implements CGI, PHP, Java Servlets or Active Server Pages (ASP), along with the application server that interacts with the database and other web objects is considered the middle tier.

3.5.2. Concepts

As mentioned earlier, content modeling builds on the concepts and methods of data modeling or object-oriented modeling. It strives to ensure that existing information is free from redundancies and reusable.

The diagram models a conference to be held on a number of topics and users who can sign into the conference and submit their papers. A paper is subject to review by three reviewers. Notice the invariant attached to the classes' paper – it ensures that authors won't be able to review their own papers.

It shows that a submitted paper will be assigned to three reviewers for review after the submission deadline has expired.

If a pre-set threshold value is reached, the paper is accepted; otherwise, it is rejected. In both cases, the authors are notified via e-mail about the outcome of the review. Finally, an accepted paper will be printed once the final version has been submitted.

3.6. HYPERTEXT MODELING

The nonlinearity of hypertext is one of the most important properties to be considered when modeling Web applications. Thus, the hypertext structure has to be designed carefully. This can be achieved by using suitable access structures, i.e., navigation options, to avoid the risk of users getting lost and putting them under excessive cognitive stress.

The objective of hypertext modeling – also known as navigation modeling – is to specify the navigability through the content of a Web application, i.e., the navigation paths available to the users. Hypertext modeling generates a two-fold result: First, it produces the hypertext structure model, also known as the navigation structure model, which defines the hypertext structure, i.e., which classes of the content model can be visited by navigation.

Second, it refines the hypertext structure model by accessing elements in the form of an access model. Hypertext modeling focuses on the structural aspects of the hypertext and the access elements. The navigational behavior of a Web application is normally not represented explicitly because it provides very little additional information for the developer.

KEYWORD

Navigation is the art and science of determining the position of a ship, plane or other vehicle, and guiding it to a specific destination.

3.6.1. Hypertext Structure Modeling Concepts

The starting point used for creating a hypertext structure model is usually the content model, which contains the classes and objects to be made available as nodes in the hypertext. The hypertext structure model is often specified as a view of the content model and is, therefore, sometimes called the navigational view.

Thereby a node is specified as a view on the content model selecting one or more objects from the content. Some methods even define transformation rules to derive links based on relationships on the content level.

An explicit design decision can add additional links. Other methods model the hypertext structure independently of the content model. For example, the OOHDM (object-oriented hypermedia design method) (Schwabe et al., 2002) offers an approach to model scenarios where the hypertext structure model can be built directly from the navigational requirements identified by these scenarios.

In any case, we can create various hypertext structure models that define hypertext views on the content. For example, if we consider the access rights of different users for the hypertext structure modeling, we can obtain personalized hypertext views.

In the reviewing system example, hypertext views are required for the following user roles: author, reviewer, and PC chair. A

PC chair can view all submitted papers. In addition, the PC chair can access the list of accepted or rejected papers and the reviewer profiles. The UML stereotype navigation class marks classes representing nodes in the hypertext structure model to distinguish them from content classes—directed associations with the stereotype navigation links.

The literature defines various specific types of links to further refine the semantics of the hypertext structure model. For example, the HDM (Hypertext Design Model) method specifies the following types of links:

- Structural links connect elements of the same node, e.g., from a review summary to the review details.
- Perspective links put various views of a node in relation to each other, e.g., the PostScript and the PDF versions of a paper.
- Application links put different nodes in relation to each other, depending on the application, e.g., a link pointing to "best paper."

Application links put different nodes in relation to each other, depending on the application, e.g., a link pointing to "best paper."

- Contextual links carry context information, e.g., the unique number of a reviewer, to navigate from one reviewer to the reviews they created.
- Non-contextual links have no associated context information, e.g., links pointing from a single review to the list of all reviews.

With regard to the distribution of nodes on the hypertext level over pages on the presentation level, WebML specifies the following types of links additionally:

- Intra-page links are used when the source and the destination of a link belonging to the same page, e.g., when a link allows the user to directly navigate to the summary of a paper displayed further down the page.
- Inter-page links are used when the source and the destination are on different pages, e.g., when detailed information about the authors and their papers are on different pages.

Based on the functional requirements of Web applications, the UWE (Koch & Kraus, 2002) modeling method defines the following types of links:

KEYWORD

PostScript is a page description language in the electronic publishing and desktop publishing realm.

Navigation links are used to navigate between nodes, e.g., links between papers and their authors.

- Process links point to the start node of a process, e.g., to the beginning of the review submission.
- External links point to a node not directly belonging to the application, e.g., to the formatting guidelines established by the publisher of the conference proceedings, which are not directly stored in the reviewing system.

The OO-H (object-oriented hypermedia) modeling method (Gomez & Cachero, 2003) defines five types of links as follows:

KEYWORD

Hypertext is text displayed on a computer display or other electronic devices with references to other text that the reader can immediately access.

- I-links (internal links) point to nodes inside the boundaries of a given navigational requirement, e.g., internal links, to review the details of one of the reviewers.
- T-links (traversal links) point to nodes covering other navigational requirements, e.g., from an author to their papers.
- R-links (requirement links) point to a start of a navigational path, e.g., to add a new review.
- X-links (external links) point to external nodes, e.g., to external formatting guidelines.
- S-links (service links) point (with their corresponding response links) to services, e.g., to an external search engine.

3.6.2. Access Modeling Concepts

The hypertext structure model built so far alone is not sufficient to describe how nodes can be reached by navigation. To allow users to navigate to nodes, the users need navigation and orientation aids. These are formulated in the form of access structures refining the hypertext structure model.

Recurring access structures are described by German & Cowan (2000); Lyardet et al. (1999); Rossi et al. (1998); Akanda & German (2005) as design patterns, also called "hypermedia design patterns" or "navigation patterns." Using these navigation patterns helps tremendously increase the quality of the hypertext model.

In our reviewing system example, if one wants to navigate from a reviewer to a paper assigned to this reviewer, one will have to identify this specific paper during navigation. For example, this could be realized in the form of a list showing all papers.

Such a selection list for navigational support is also known as an "index." An index is an access structure that allows users to select a single object (i.e., one object of the content) out of a homogeneous list of objects. In contrast, a menu allows users to access heterogeneous nodes or further menus (i.e., submenus).

Other access structures are the guided tour and the query. A guided tour allows users to sequentially walk through a number of nodes. A query allows users to search for nodes. Most modeling methods offer dedicated model elements for the most frequently used navigation patterns.

Special navigation patterns include home, which points to the home page of a Web application, and landmark, which points to a node that can be reached from within all nodes.

Some access structures can be automatically added to the hypertext structure model (Koch & Kraus, 2002). For example, indexes can be added automatically whenever we want to allow access to a set (>1) of objects of a node.

KEYWORD

Marketing tactics are the actual strategic actions that direct the promotion of a product or service to influence specific marketing goals.

3.6.3. Relation to Content Modeling

Depending on the underlying modeling method, the hypertext model is more or less strongly dependent on the content model. There exists both a dependence at the type of level, e.g., which classes in the content model form which node in the hypertext model, and at the instance level, i.e., which sets of objects in the content model populate that node in the hypertext model.

Not all methods exactly describe dependencies between the content and hypertext models. Nevertheless, some methods specify a direct derivation of the hypertext from the content by defining nodes based on views (in the sense of "database views") (Schwabe et al., 2002; Koch & Kraus, 2002).

3.7. CHALLENGES AND RELATED WORK

One of the interesting challenges of web software is that it has been discovered to have very high-quality requirements. Since user expectations and business realities have conspired to make excellent quality rarely profitable, a large portion of the software industry has been able to thrive with relatively low quality requirements. A combination of time-to-market and marketing tactics has virtually always determined the competitiveness of traditional software products. However, brand loyalty (also known as "site loyalty") for web apps seems to be minimal to nonexistent.

This means that if company A launches a website first and company B enters the market later, users would swiftly switch to company B's website if they believe it to be of greater quality. In other words, being "later and better" is frequently preferable than "sooner but worse."

This places a great deal of responsibility on the web software's designers, developers, and testers to guarantee that it demonstrates extremely high reliability, usability, and security. Compared to most "conventional" software, these quality factors will significantly negatively influence firm profits.

Remember

The hypertext structure has to be designed carefully. This can be achieved by using suitable access structures, i.e., navigation options, to avoid the risk of users getting lost and putting them under excessive cognitive stress.

There are additional factors. For instance, a corner medicine shop ("brick and mortar") might anticipate neighborhood customers Monday through Saturday, 8:00 AM to 7:00 PM, whereas a web-based company can anticipate clients from all over the world.

It may only be mid-afternoon in Beijing, despite it being three in the morning in Virginia. Web sites, therefore, need to be exceedingly available—not just 24 hours a day, but 365 days a year. Unlike shrink-wrapped software programs, web-based applications don't need to be sold or distributed when upgrades are made, which is another significant distinction.

This, together with the quick advancement of technology, makes maintainability essential for web applications. Finally, in contrast to traditional businesses, whose potential customers are typically limited by physical concerns such as geography and traffic, the growth of web-based businesses has unlimited potential because there are currently hundreds of millions of users on the web, each of whom is only a click away and is therefore "in the neighborhood" of the store. This necessitates that web software be extremely scalable and equipped for rapid growth in the number of servers, services, and users.

To ensure the quality of traditional programs, a great deal of work has gone into developing testing methodologies for both standalone and distributed systems. Despite the fact that some of these strategies can be utilized to improve the quality of web apps, certain of their unique characteristics and needs prohibit them from being immediately adopted. These challenges are summarized below:

- Despite many similarities in their basic architecture, there is a significant distinction between client-server systems and web applications. The roles that clients and servers play in traditional client-server systems are specified and rigid.

However, client-side programs and contents may be dynamically produced in web applications. For instance, a server might deliver a dynamically produced HTML file, including links, JavaScripts, and contents. This means that the past inputs impact how the client and server interact later.

- Correctness and efficiency are typically the most crucial quality parameters for conventional systems. Other quality features can frequently be more crucial for web apps, but we don't have many methods for supporting them.

For instance, interoperability and compatibility issues are urgent and more significant than they are with traditional systems. Traditional programs have very few conflicts and changes since they are created for a specific predetermined, well-understood environment.

KEYWORD

WiFi is a wireless technology used to connect computers, tablets, smartphones and other devices to the internet.

Web applications are frequently impacted by elements that could lead to compatibility and interoperability problems. For instance, distinct web server packages, such as IIS from Microsoft, Apache, Web Logic from IBM, and others, can run on many operating systems, including UNIX, Linux, Windows, MacOS, and AIX, each of which has multiple versions.

The situation is much more complicated on the client side because there are numerous operating systems and various web browser versions. Customers can also choose from a variety of connection methods, including dial-up modems, wifi, direct internet access, and ISPs.

It is more difficult to create web application components that are compatible with one another, and that interoperate appropriately and readily as a result of all this heterogeneity.

- The variance in the control of the application's execution is another distinction between web apps and other sorts of programs. In conventional systems, the control flow is entirely controlled by the program; the user does not influence it.

Users have the ability to alter the standard control flow of a web application while running it without informing the program controller. For example, users can press the back or refresh button in the web browser, which totally changes the execution context, causing unexpected results. Furthermore, changes in the client-side configuration may affect the behavior of web applications. For example, users can turn off cookies, which can cause subsequent operations to malfunction.

KEYWORD

Client-server is a relationship in which one program, the client, requests a service or resource from another program, the server.

- Web applications also have much faster maintenance requirements than most traditional software. Web technologies evolve more rapidly than traditional software technologies, and the changes in web application requirements are also more dramatic.

Therefore, maintenance not only needs to be done more frequently but needs to be done more efficiently due to the peculiar time-to-market pressure for web applications.

- Web applications also have features that are not present in client-server and distributed systems. These include session control, cookies, the stateless aspect of HTTP, and new security issues. Therefore, new solutions are necessary for these special features.

SUMMARY

- **Modeling Web-based Applications:** This part of the chapter summarizes Modeling in web-based applications. The different models are – the analysis model, web applications, and web services. Challenges and related work of modeling web applications have also been discussed in this chapter.
- **Model Driven Design of Web Applications:** In this part of the chapter, different model driven design has been discussed they are – running example, data model, and hypertext model. Integrating business processes and web application development have also been explained in this chapter.
- **Modeling Requirements:** The end of the chapter summarizes the modeling requirements, content modeling its objectives and concepts, hypertext modeling – hypertext structure modeling concepts, Access modeling concept, and relation to content modeling.

REVIEW QUESTIONS

1. Explain modeling web-based applications?
2. What are the challenges and related work in modeling web applications?
3. What is the model driven design of web applications?
4. What are the modeling requirements in web applications?
5. What are the objectives and concepts of content modeling?
6. What is hypertext modeling?
7. What are hypertext structure modeling concepts?
8. What are access modeling concepts?

MULTIPLE CHOICE QUESTIONS

1. Which of the following characteristics should not be used to assess the quality of a Web App?

a. Esthetics
b. Reliability
c. Maintainability
d. Usability

2. Which of the following are the design goals for every web app?

a. Simplicity
b. Consistency

c. Navigability
d. All of the above

3. Which of the following are Web app interaction mechanisms?

a. Graphic icons
b. Graphic images
c. Navigation menus
d. All of the above

4. A study of an existing system refers to:

a. System analysis
b. System design
c. System testing
d. None

5. _________________ is a mechanism for collecting domain knowledge in a way that allows it to be reapplied when a new problem is encountered.

a. Software design
b. Software patterns
c. Software testing
d. All of the above

Answers to Multiple Choice Questions

1. (a) 2. (d) 3. (d) 4. (b) 5. (b)

REFERENCES

1. Alalfi, M. H., Cordy, J. R., & Dean, T. R., (2008). *Modeling Methods for Web Application Verification and Testing: State of the Art*. www.research.cs.queensu.ca. John Wiley & Sons. Available at: https://research.cs.queensu.ca/home/cordy/Papers/ACD_STVR_Survey.pdf (accessed on 04 March 2023).
2. Brambilla, M., (2014). Process modeling in web applications. *ACM Transactions on Software Engineering and Methodology (TOSEM)*. academia. Available at: https://www.academia.edu/2849672/Process_modeling_in_web_applications (accessed on 04 March 2023).
3. Brambilla, M., Ceri, S., & Fraternali, P., (2006). *Process Modeling in Web Applications.* www.pages.saclay.inria.fr. ACM. Available at: http://pages.saclay.inria.fr/ioana.manolescu/PAPERS/BrambillaCFM-TOSEM2006.pdf (accessed on 04 March 2023).

4. Brambilla, M., et al., (2006). Process modeling in web applications. *ACM Transactions on Software Engineering and Methodology, 15*(4), 360–409. Available at: https://doi.org/10.1145/1178625.1178627.

5. Schwinger, W., & Koch, N., (2006). *modeling Web Applications.* www.csun.edu.twang. Available at: https://www.csun.edu/~twang/595WEB/Slides/WebAppsModeling.pdf (accessed on 04 March 2023).

6. Schwinger, W., & Koch, N., (2006). *modeling Web Applications.* www.researchgate.net. Wiley & Sons. Available at: https://www.researchgate.net/publication/200827803_Modeling_Web_Applications (accessed on 04 March 2023).

7. Wu, Y., & Offutt, J., (n.d). *Modeling and Testing Web-Based Applications.* www.cs.albany.edu. Information and Software Engineering Department George Mason University. Available at: https://www.cs.albany.edu/~mhc/csi668/05S/paper3.pdf (accessed on 04 March 2023).

CHAPTER 4

WEB APPLICATION ARCHITECTURES

UNIT INTRODUCTION

In the current chapter, we will extend our discussion on web application architectures (WAA), the meaning of architectures, developing architectures, and categorizing architectures. The pervasive web application architecture, application scenarios, TCP/IP, and data-aspect architectures will also be explained towards the end of the chapter.

The World Wide Web was first intended as a system for exchanging documents. These documents could simply be published and connected to form the web, which is a collection of interconnected web pages. Users found web pages to be very appealing due to their immediate nature and ease of access, which helped the internet, become popular very quickly.

But it soon became clear that the web, as a platform for applications, offers much more than just serving as a document database. It was imminent that people would be interested in sending functional software over the internet and running it in a browser.

User interaction was initially incorporated into web sites utilizing rendering techniques that allowed for the dynamic construction of web pages. This allowed for simple interactions, including the usage of forms and server-side programming, as well as dynamic client-side capabilities. Even though these websites weren't really web applications back then, a shift from simple web pages to actual web applications had begun. Web applications have advanced significantly in many ways. Compared to early online apps, the user experience is significantly better in today's modern web applications, and the functionality offered is vastly increased.

The standards—specifically HTML5 and the associated APIs (such as Web workers, Web storage, micro-data, and canvas)—have developed over time to better support web applications, and browser vendors have invested in transforming their products from simple document viewers into true application platforms.

Recently, we have also witnessed the rise of platforms like Firefox OS (formerly known as Boot to Gecko), where the browser environment serves as the operating system and where so-called native applications are created using web technologies.

This has all led to the development of web applications that are responsive, dynamic, and feature rich. In other words, they have a lot of features that we are familiar with from desktop applications. JavaScript is increasingly being used to create huge and complicated applications rather than just as a pocket knife to add a feature to a web page quickly.

Web apps are now considered to be incredibly difficult to create and maintain. They are supposed to perform equally effectively across various contexts, including desktop and mobile browsers in which they are run.

Additionally, given the history of web apps, it should not come as a huge surprise that their limitations are caused by an environment that was not initially intended for them. The development environment and tools would probably be different today if web standards and browsers had been created from the ground up to support web applications rather than web pages.

The ongoing evolution of the web platform makes it difficult to include any overarching norms or principles for creating online apps, which is another challenging element. As a result, programmers are at the frameworks' mercy, which creates new issues.

There are several frameworks available, and each one has its own set of trade-offs with regard to performance, security, supplied conventions, and the development paradigm as a whole. Different frameworks are useful for different purposes, and many differ considerably in how they direct or even require the development model.

Programmers may not always understand the trade-offs and dangers that frameworks pose. Additionally, programmers depend on the frameworks and rely on the utilities they offer, oblivious to or unaware of what is really going on underneath. Numerous frameworks also support a close coupling of the client and server components. The reuse of code and programmers' skill sets is extremely challenging due to this type of coupling.

There is a lot of flexibility for the programmer to design the application in many ways, even with an appropriate framework for a certain purpose. The application logic's fragmentation is a nice illustration of this.

On the one hand, it is fragmented between the client-side components running in the browser and the server-side components running in the server. On the other hand, it is fragmented over various technologies, including a variety of programming languages and presentation templates that can all be utilized to accomplish the application logic.

Further, the server and client communication channels are also quite flexible. The programmer must decide how to use it and what data should be delivered in different circumstances. Because of all this complexity, the programming environment is not only tough for newcomers to adjust to and learn in but also full of performance, security, and maintainability hazards.

Granted, a good framework can simplify things for the developer, but this does not solve the fundamental issues of code fragmentation and a lack of established norms. In order to address the issues preventing modern web development, it is necessary to embrace web and HTTP rather than adding leaky abstractions to them.

Learning Objectives

Following the completion of the chapter, the students should be able to understand the following:

- Understand what architecture are and its types – developing architecture and categorizing architecture;
- Understand pervasive web application architecture;
- Understand the application scenarios;
- Learn how to build web applications in one easy lesson;
- Understand what TCP/IP is;
- Understand the specifics of web application architectures (WAA);
- Understand data aspect architectures.

Key Terms

- Architectures
- Categorizing
- Pervasive
- Scenario
- Transmission
- Specifics
- Application

4.1. FUNDAMENTALS OF ARCHITECTURE

4.1.1. What Is Architecture?

There is no unique definition of the term "architecture." For instance, the renowned Carnegie-Mellon University Software Engineering Institute (SEI) home page lists more than 20 variations of the phrase. Instead of introducing yet another variety, we attempt to outline the key characteristics of software architectures (as stated by Starke, 2002):

KEYWORD

Architecture is the art and science of designing buildings and other physical structures.

- **Architecture Describes Structure:** According to Bass et al. (1998), the architecture of a software system consists of its structures, the breakdown into components, and their interfaces and interactions. It can be regarded as a building design and flowchart for a software product because it describes both the static and dynamic components of that software system.
- **Architecture Forms the Transition from Analysis to Implementation:** We attempt to iteratively divide the functional requirements and quality requirements into software components, their relationships, and their interfaces when creating architecture. A variety of methods, including the Unified Process, facilitate this process.
- **Architecture can be Looked at from Different Viewpoints:** Depending on the perspective from which architecture is viewed, we can highlight and list many architectural features. We typically distinguish between four different viewpoints (*see also* Kruchten, 1995; Hofmeister et al., 1995):
  - The conceptual view, which outlines the application domain's constituent entities and their connections;
  - The runtime view, which details the system's running components, such as servers or communication links.
  - The process view maps processes at system runtime while considering synchronization and concurrency.; and
  - The implementation view describes the software artifacts of the system, such as its components, subsystems, or source code. Modeling languages, like the unified modeling language (UML), facilitate this division into distinct points of view.

- **Architecture Makes a System Understandable:** We may better manage the complexity of software systems by structuring them and dissecting them from various angles, making the systems more understandable. The abstraction of system components also makes it easier to communicate significant architectural challenges.

Architecture represents the framework for a flexible system: According to Tom DeMarco (1995), architecture is a "framework of change," meaning that the software architecture creates the framework for a software system's evolution. Extensions of a system will, at best, be challenging to implement if they are not anticipated in advance.

TIPS

The roots of Web technology can be found in the original internet protocols (known collectively as TCP/IP), developed in the 1980s.

4.1.2. Developing Architectures

Software's requirements, and thus its architecture, are dynamic. During and after the development of an application, technical and organizational restrictions change. This could result from imprecise requirements at the start of the development process or revised needs once a system is finished. As such, software systems are frequently referred to as "moving targets."

Functional needs, or the services a system offers, and quality factors like scalability or performance are the main factors that affect the architecture of an application. In addition to these needs, technological constraints can impact architectures.

These limits might be caused by the operating system, middleware (e.g., a CORBA implementation), standards, integrating legacy systems, coding standards, distribution issues, or the system software itself (e.g., the distribution over different company locations). The software architect's experiences also play a significant part in the definition of architecture.

Architectures are generally built iteratively since software systems are dynamic targets. With this strategy, the risks brought on by unsecured requirements and restrictions should be calculable and manageable. However, using an iterative process does not ensure a good architecture. For example, while developing architecture, an iterative method is insufficient for resolving specific design issues like integrating a legacy system. Fortunately, design patterns have been demonstrated to be extremely helpful in supporting such design choices.

4.1.2.1. Patterns

Patterns highlight recurrent design issues that develop in a particular design context and offer answers (*see* Gamma et al., 1997; Buschmann et al., 1996, 2000). A solution outlines the contributing elements, their roles, their connections, and how they interact with each other to solve the particular problem.

Thus, patterns allow us to reuse tested and collected design knowledge, assisting in the creation of high-quality software systems. Buschmann et al. (1996) identify patterns on three different abstraction levels:

- **Architecture Patterns:** These patterns map the basic structuring processes for software systems. They outline the roles, connections, and interactions of architectural subsystems. Model-view-controller (MVC) is one example of this kind of pattern.
- **Design Patterns:** These patterns describe parts' organization, connections, and interaction to address a design issue in a particular situation. Design patterns are abstract from a particular computer language, although they operate within the framework of architecture patterns. An example of a design pattern is the Publisher-Subscriber pattern described by Buschmann et al. (1996).
- **Idioms:** Identify design patterns that pertain to a particular programming language implementation, such as the Counted-Pointer idiom for storage management in C++ (Buschmann et al., 1996).

KEYWORD

Model–view–controller (MVC) is a software design pattern commonly used for developing user interfaces that divides the related program logic into three interconnected elements.

Patterns are available for various infrastructures, including J2EE and CORBA (Malveau & Mowbray, 1997).

However, patterns can only serve as a general direction for the current issue. The software architect must modify patterns for each problem and set of restrictions. The architect must also integrate and fine-tune the patterns being employed. Buschmann et al. (2000) suggest using so-called pattern languages to facilitate the integration process.

A pattern language offers multiple purposes for patterns, provides different ways to apply them, and demonstrates the adjustments required to ensure a sound system. A pattern language example for distributed systems is provided by Buschmann et al. (2000). Architecture patterns for commercial applications are discussed in their patterns for e-business (IBM, 2002), along with how they can be translated to the IBM infrastructure. These architectural designs are improved along a decision-making process that extends from the use case to the target architecture.

4.1.2.2. Frameworks

Frameworks offer yet another way to reuse previously acquired architectural knowledge. A framework is a reusable software system having pre-built general functionality. An application that is ready to use can be created using the framework (*see also* Fayad et al., 1999).

The framework acts as a model for a given application area's fundamental design and functionalities. This indicates that the architectural expertise found in a framework can be fully incorporated into the application.

However, the advantages of a framework, such as the ease of reusing architecture and functionality, must be weighed against its drawbacks, such as a significant amount of training effort, a lack of standards for integrating different frameworks, and the associated reliance on manufacturers.

ACTIVITY 4.1.

Web App Planning-Out Sourcing: A substantial percentage of web app is outsourced to venders who (purportedly) specialized in the development of web-based systems and applications. In such cases, customers ask for a fixed price quote for web- based systems and applications. In such cases, customers ask for a fixed price quote for web app development from two or more vendors, evaluate competing quotes, and then select a vendor to do the work.

Initiate the Project: If outsourcing is the strategy to be chosen for web app development, an organization must perform a number of tasks before searching for an outsourcing vendor to do the work.

4.1.3. Categorizing Architectures

Over the past few years, numerous designs have been developed for various requirements across various application domains. The layering aspect of architectures or the support of various data and data formats – the data part of architectures – is discussed by Anastopoulos & Romberg (2001) and Bongio et al.'s (2003) descriptions of architectures for web application environments:

- **Layering Aspect:** It refers to a system's organizational structure in several stages to implement the idea of "separation of concerns" within a software system. Many frameworks in the field of distributed systems and Web applications are primarily structured by the layering aspect, for example, J2EE (Sun Microsystems, 2003a). Enterprise application integration (EAI), which is the term for architectures used to integrate legacy systems, and portals, also fall under this category.
- **Data Aspect:** Data can be structured or non-structured. Structured data, such as tables in a relational database or XML structures in a document, adhere to a defined pattern. Multimedia content without a clear organization, such as photos, audio, and video, is considered non-structured data. Their automatic processing is challenging as a result.

KEYWORD

Software system consists of several separate computer programs and associated configuration files, documentation, etc., that operate together.

As software systems are distributed more widely, designs and infrastructures handling the distribution of data and messages have been developed.

- **Distributed Object Middleware (DOM):** Accessing remote objects is made possible by this kind of infrastructure. This technique is based on the remote procedure call (RPC) protocol. Some DOM systems additionally permit object interactivity across several platforms (e.g., CORBA). Microsoft's DCOM (distributed component object model) and Sun Microsystems' EJB (Enterprise Java Beans) are two further instances of this kind of technology.
- **Virtual Shared Memory (VSM):** Using the VSM concept, distributed processes can access shared data. The processes themselves access a shared memory. A suitable middleware that is transparent to the processes is used to distribute the data. Since it is "virtual," this data can be "anywhere" in the system. The VSM systems Corso and Equip are two examples.
- **Message Oriented Middleware (MOM):** These systems include features for asynchronous message transfer. In contrast to synchronous communication, asynchronous communication sends messages to the recipient regardless of the recipient's availability, i.e., whether the recipient is online or offline. MOM ensures the delivery of messages. Examples of MOM systems include Sun's JMS (Java Messaging Service) and Microsoft's MSMQ (Microsoft Message Queue).

- **Peer-to-Peer (P2P):** It refers to point-to-point connections used for point-to-point communication between two devices (the peers) in a system without using a server. Peers are essentially on par with one another P2P systems explain how devices in a network of this type connect with and "find" one another. Examples of P2P systems include JXTA and X middle.
- **Service Oriented Middleware (SOM):** This improves DOM systems by the concept of services. A variety of objects and their behaviors constitute a service in this context. These objects employ a specified interface to open a service to other systems and services. A straightforward integration of services across platform boundaries is supported by SOM, which defines communication protocols between services and offers location- and migration-transparent access to services. One example of a SOM is Sun's Jini system.

4.2. PERVASIVE WEB APPLICATION ARCHITECTURE

A web application is a program that can be accessed through a network, such as the Internet or an intranet. The phrase may also refer to a computer program that is written in a language that is supported by browsers (like JavaScript, along with a markup language that is rendered by browsers, like HTML) and that depends on a widely used web browser to make the program executable.

Web browsers are widely used, and utilizing one as a client, sometimes known as a thin client, is convenient, contributing to web applications' popularity. One of the main factors contributing to the popularity of web applications is their inherent support for cross-platform compatibility.

Another is the ease with which they can be updated and maintained without distributing and installing software on potentially thousands of client machines. Webmail, online shopping, auctions, wikis, and many other features are typical web applications.

Through Java, JavaScript, DHTML, Flash, Silver light, and other technologies, application specific methods such as drawing on the screen, playing audio, and accessing the keyboard and mouse are all possible.

Many services have worked to combine all of these into a more familiar interface that adopts the appearance of an operating system.

KEYWORD

Communication protocols are formal descriptions of digital message formats and rules.

These technologies also support general purpose techniques such as drag and drop.

Web developers often use client-side scripting to add functionality, especially to create an interactive experience that does not require page reloading. Recently, technologies have been developed to coordinate client-side scripting with server-side technologies such as PHP.

Ajax, a web development technique using a combination of various technologies, is an example of technology that creates a more interactive experience (Figure 4.1).

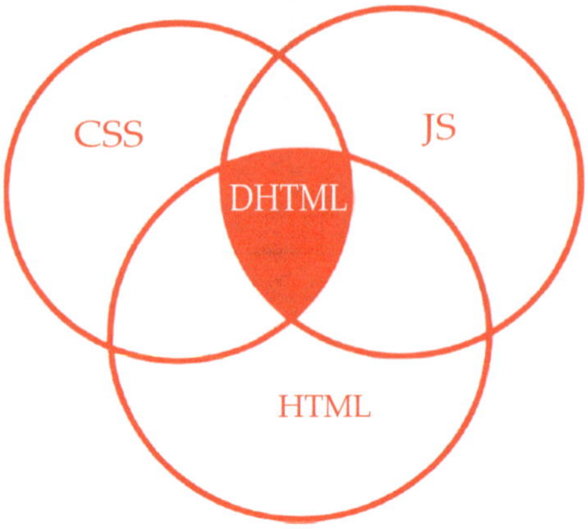

Figure 4.1. *DHTML schema.*

Source: Image by Wikimedia Commons.

4.2.1. Structure

Applications are usually broken into logical chunks called "tiers," where every tier is assigned a role. Traditional applications consist only of 1 tier, which resides on the client machine, but web applications lend themselves to an n-tiered approach by nature.

Though many variations are possible, the most common structure is the three-tiered application. In its most common form, the three tiers are called presentation, application, and storage, in this order.

A web browser is the first tier (presentation), an engine using some dynamic Web content technology (such as ASP, ASP.NET, CGI, ColdFusion, JSP/Java, PHP, Perl, Python, Ruby on Rails or Struts2) is the middle tier (application logic), and a database is the third tier (storage).

The web browser sends requests to the middle tier, which services them by making queries and updates against the database and generates a user interface. For more complex applications, a 3-tier solution may fall short, and it may be beneficial to use an n-tiered approach, where the greatest benefit is breaking the business logic, which resides on the application tier, into a more fine-grained model.

Another benefit may be adding an integration tier that separates the data tier from the rest of the tiers by providing an easy-to-use interface to access the data. For example, the client data would be accessed by calling a "list_clients ()" function instead of making an SQL query directly against the client table on the database. This allows the underlying database to be replaced without changing the other tiers.

TIPS

The generator uses the SAX parser to read the XML document, and then generates SAX messages, called events.

Some see a web application as a two-tier architecture. This can be a "smart" client that performs all the work and queries a "dumb" server or a "dumb" client that relies on a "smart" server. The client would handle the presentation tier, the server would have the database (storage tier), and the business logic (application tier) would be on one of them or on both.

While this increases the scalability of the applications and separates the display and the database, it still doesn't allow for true specialization of layers, so most applications will outgrow this model.

4.3. HOW TO BUILD WEB APPLICATIONS IN ONE EASY LESSON?

But what does it mean to design a Web application, as contrasted to a Web page or a Web site? Each level of Web design has its own techniques and its own set of issues.

4.3.1. Web Page Design Resources

For web page design, there is a variety of books available. Beyond the tutorial books that purport to teach HTML, JavaScript, and CGI scripting overnight, some good books discuss the deeper issues associated with designing Web pages.

One of the better choices is The Non-Designer's Web Book by Robin Williams (not the comedian). Williams' books are full of useful information and guidelines for those constructing Web pages, especially those not explicitly schooled in design or typography.

4.3.2. Web Site Design Resources

When it comes to Web sites, there are far fewer resources available. Information Architecture for the World Wide Web, by Louis Rosenfeld and Peter Morville, was one of the rare books covering the issues of designing Web sites as opposed to Web pages. It is, unfortunately, out of print.

Remember

According to Bass et al. (1998), the architecture of a software system consists of its structures, the decomposition into components, and their interfaces and relationships.

4.3.3. Web Application Design Resources

When we examined the current literature available on the subject of web application development, we found there were three main categories of books currently available:

- **Technical Overviews:** The first category is the technical overview. These books are usually at a very high level, describing terminology and technology in broad terms. They do not go into enough detail to enable the reader to design and build serious Web applications.

They are most often intended for 'managers' and 'executives' who want a surface understanding of the terminology without going too deeply into specific application development issues. Frequently, they attempt to cover technology in huge brushstrokes so that you see books whose focus is simply 'Java,' 'XML,' or 'The Web.'

- **In-Depth Technical Resources:** The second category comprises in-depth technical resources for developing Web applications using specific platforms. The books in this category provide in-depth coverage of very narrow areas, concentrating on the 'how-to' of using a particular language or platform without explaining what is going on 'under the hood.'

While such books may be useful in teaching programmers to develop applications for a specific platform, they provide little or no information about the underlying technologies, focusing instead on the platform-specific implementation of those technologies.

Should developers be called upon to rewrite an application for another platform, the knowledge they acquired from reading these books would rarely be transferable to that new platform.

Given that Web technology changes so rapidly, today's platform of choice is tomorrow's outdated legacy system. When new development platforms emerge, developers without a fundamental understanding of the inner workings of Web applications have to learn their inner workings from the ground up because they lack an understanding of first principles—of what the systems they wrote really did. Thus, the ability to use fundamental technological knowledge across platforms is critical.

- **These Form a Third Category:** Such books are useful, naturally, as references, but not to learn about the technology. We found a book lacking an in-depth examination of the basic concepts and general principles of Web application development.

Such a book would cover the core protocols and technologies of the Internet in depth, imparting the principles associated with writing applications for the Web. It would use examples from specific technologies (e.g., CGI scripts and Servlets) but would not promote or endorse particular platforms.

Too often, developers with proficiency only within a specific application development platform (like active server pages (ASP), cold fusion, PHP, or Perl CGI scripting) cannot transfer that proficiency directly to another platform.

Only through a fundamental understanding of the core technology can developers be expected to grow with the rapid technological changes associated with Web application development.

KEYWORD

Application development platform is a set of integrated technologies that enable teams to build software applications efficiently.

4.3.4. Principles of Web Application Design

What do we mean when we discuss the general principles that need to be understood to properly design and develop Web applications? We mean the core set of protocols and languages associated with Web applications.

This includes HTTP (Hypertext Transfer Protocol) and HTML (Hypertext Markup Language), which are fundamental to creating and transmitting Web pages. It also includes the older Internet protocols like Telnet and FTP, protocols used for message transfer like SMTP and IMAP, plus advanced protocols and languages like XML.

Additionally, it includes knowledge of databases and multimedia presentations since many sophisticated Web applications use these technologies extensively. In some sense, the ideal Web application architect must be a 'jack of all trades.' People who design Web applications must understand HTTP and HTML and the other underlying Internet protocols. They must be familiar with JavaScript, XML, relational databases, graphic design, and multimedia.

They must be well versed in application server technology and have a strong background in information architecture. Please let us know if you find people with all these qualifications—we would love to hire them! Rare is the person who cannot only architect a Web site but also design the graphics, create the database schema, produce the multimedia programs, and configure the e-commerce transactions.

In the absence of such a Web application superhero/guru/demigod, the best you can hope for is a person who at least understands the issues associated with designing Web applications. Someone who understands the underlying languages and protocols supporting such applications.

Someone who can understand the mechanisms for providing access to a database and multimedia information through a Web application, we hope that, by reading this book, you can acquire the skills needed to design and build complex applications for the World Wide Web.

TIPS

A "smart" client that performs all the work and queries a "dumb" server, or a "dumb" client that relies on a "smart" server.

No, there is no 'one easy lesson' for learning the ins and outs of designing Web applications. However, this book will hopefully enable you to design and build sophisticated Web applications that are scalable, maintainable, extensible, and reusable.

We examine various approaches to the process of Web application development—starting with the CGI approach, looking at template languages like Cold Fusion and ASP, and working our way up to the Java Enterprise (J2EE) approach. However, at each level, we concentrate not on the particular development platform but on the considerations associated with designing and building Web applications regardless of the underlying platform.

4.4. BEFORE THE WEB: TCP/IP

The roots of Web technology can be found in the original Internet protocols (known collectively as TCP/IP) developed in the 1980s. These protocols were an outgrowth of work done for the United States Defense Department to design the ARPANET network.

The ARPANET was named for ARPA, the Advanced Research Projects Agency of the United States Department of Defense.

It came into being due to efforts funded by the Department of Defense in the 1970s to develop an open, common, distributed, and decentralized computer networking architecture.

There were a number of problems with existing network architectures that the Defense Department wanted to resolve. First and foremost was the centralized nature of existing networks. At that time, the typical network topology was centralized.

A computer network has a single point of control directing communication between all the systems belonging to that network. From a military perspective, such a topology had a critical flaw: Destroy that central point of control, and all communication possibilities were lost. Another issue was the proprietary nature of existing network architectures.

Most were developed and controlled by private corporations, who had a vested interest both in pushing their own products and in keeping their technology to themselves. Further, the proprietary nature of the technology limited the interoperability between different systems.

It was important, even then, to ensure that the mechanisms for communicating across computer networks were not proprietary or controlled in any way by private interests, lest the entire network becomes dependent on the whims of a single corporation.

Thus, the Defense Department funded an endeavor to design the protocols for the next generation of computer communications networking architectures. Establishing a decentralized, distributed network topology was foremost among the design goals for the new networking architecture.

Such a topology would allow communications to continue, for the most part, undisrupted, even if anyone's system was damaged or destroyed. In such a topology, the network 'intelligence' would not reside in a single point of control. Instead, it would be distributed among many systems throughout the network.

To facilitate this (and to accommodate other network reliability considerations), they employed a packet-switching technology, whereby a network 'message' could be split into packets, each of which might take a different route over the network, arrive in completely mixed-up order, and still be reassembled and understood by the intended recipient. The protocols needed to be open to promote interoperability: be readily available to anyone who wanted

KEYWORD

Network topology is the physical and logical arrangement of nodes and connections in a network.

to connect their system to the network. An infrastructure was needed to design the set of agreed-upon protocols and to formulate new protocols for new technologies that might be added to the network in the future.

An internet working group (INWG) was formed to examine the issues associated with connecting heterogeneous networks together in an open, uniform manner. This group provided an open platform for proposing, debating, and approving protocols.

The INWG evolved over time into other bodies, like the IAB (Internet Activities Board, later renamed the Internet Architecture Board), the IANA (Internet Assigned Numbers Authority), and later, the IETF (Internet Engineering Task Force) and IESG (Internet Engineering Steering Group).

These bodies defined the standards that 'govern' the Internet. They established the formal processes for proposing new protocols, discussing and debating the merits of these proposals, and ultimately approving them as accepted Internet standards.

Proposals for new protocols (or updated versions of existing protocols) are provided as Requests for Comments, also known as RFCs. Once approved, the RFCs are treated as the standard documentation for the new or updated protocol.

4.5. TCP/IP

The original ARPANET was the first fruit borne of this endeavor. The protocols behind the ARPANET evolved over time into the TCP/IP Protocol Suite, a layered taxonomy of data communications protocols (Figure 4.2).

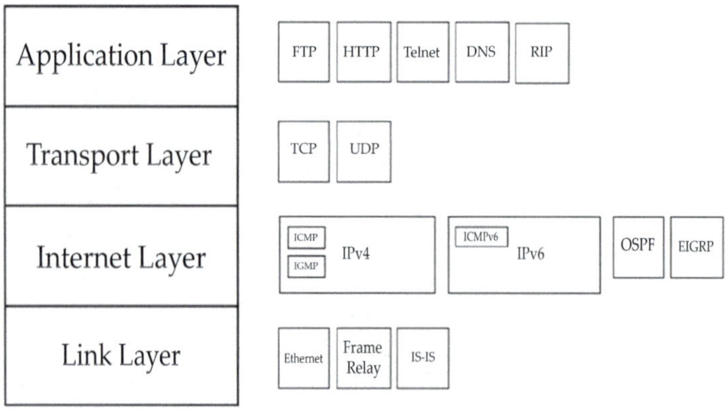

Figure 4.2. *TCP/IP model.*

Source: Image by Wikimedia Commons.

The name TCP/IP refers to two of the most important protocols within the suite: TCP (transmission control protocol) and IP (internet protocol). Still, the suite is comprised of many other significant protocols and services.

4.5.1. Layers

The protocol layers associated with TCP/IP (above the 'layer' of physical interconnection) are:

- The network interface layer;
- The internet layer;
- The transport layer; and
- The application layers.

Because this protocol taxonomy contains layers, implementations of these protocols are often known as a protocol stack. The Network Interface layer is the layer responsible for the lowest level of data transmission within TCP/IP, facilitating communication with the underlying physical network.

KEYWORD

Internet layer is responsible for logical transmission of data packets over the internet.

The Internet layer provides the mechanisms for intersystem communications, controlling message routing, validity checking, and message header composition/decomposition. The protocol known as IP (which stands, oddly enough, for Internet Protocol) operates on this layer, as does ICMP (the Internet Control Message Protocol).

ICMP handles the transmission of control and error messages between systems. Ping is an Internet service that operates through ICMP. The Transport layer provides message transport services between applications running on remote systems.

This is the layer in which TCP (transmission control protocol) operates. TCP provides reliable, connection-oriented message transport. Most of the well-known Internet services make use of TCP as their foundation. However, some services that do not require the reliability (and overhead) associated with TCP use UDP (which stands for user datagram protocol).

For instance, streaming audio and video services would gladly sacrifice a few lost packets to get faster performance out of their data streams. Hence, these services often operate over UDP, which trades reliability for performance. The Application layer is the highest level within the TCP/IP protocol stack. It is within this layer that most of the services we associate with 'the Internet' operate.

These Internet services provided some degree of information exchange. Still, it took the birth of the web to bring those initial dreams to fruition in a way that the earliest developers of these services might never have imagined.

Remember

It is easy to imagine that in the future clients using mobile devices will generate a large percentage of all Web service requests.

4.5.2. The Client/Server Paradigm

TCP/IP applications tend to operate according to the client/server paradigm. This simply means that, in these applications, servers (also called services and daemons, depending on the language of the underlying operating system) execute by (1) waiting for requests from client programs to arrive and then (2) processing those requests. Client programs can be applications used by human beings, or they could be servers that need to make their own requests that other servers can only fulfill. More often than not, the client and server run on separate machines and communicate via a connection across a network.

Early implementations of client/server architectures did not use open protocols. What this meant was that client programs needed to be as 'heavy' as the server programs. A 'lightweight' client (also called a thin client) could only exist in a framework where common protocols and application controls were associated with the client machine's operating system. Without such a framework, many of the connectivity features had to be included directly into the client program, adding to its weight. One advantage of using TCP/IP for client/server applications was that the protocol stack was installed on the client machine as part of the operating system, and the client program itself could be more of a thin client.

Web applications are a prime example of the employment of thin clients in applications. Rather than building a custom program to perform desired application tasks, web applications use the web browser, a program that is already installed on most users' systems. You cannot create a client much thinner than a program that users have already installed on their desktops!

4.6. SPECIFICS OF WEB APPLICATION ARCHITECTURES (WAA)

One remarkable development concerns the quality requirements for Web applications. We can see that Web application requirements are more demanding than requirements for comparable traditional software systems. This development, especially regarding changeability, performance, security, scalability, and availability, has encouraged the proposal and introduction of specific technical infrastructures for the development and operation of Web applications.

Thus, we have to distinguish web infrastructure architecture on the one hand and web application architecture on the other. Jablonski et al. (2004) refer to the former as web platform architectures (WPA) and the latter as WAA.

As WAA strongly depends on the problem domain a web application is in, this chapter will focus primarily on WPAs. WPA has been developed for a wide variety of problems. Application servers, like implementations of the J2EE (Sun Microsystems, 2003a) and the .NET platform (Beer et al., 2003), try to provide basic services for session handling, protocol wrapping, and data access.

Besides application servers, specific architectural solutions have been developed for security, performance, and data integration issues. Examples of these are firewalls, caching proxies, and EAI, respectively.

KEYWORD

Data integration is the process of combining data from different sources into a single, unified view.

Paradoxically, using this wide range of systems has made evaluating and maintaining distinct quality requirements increasingly difficult. For example, meeting performance requirements become more difficult due to the increasing number of components and products used by third-party (commercial or open source) vendors.

Other problems in the development of Web applications are the homogeneity and immaturity of technical infrastructures. Gorton & Liu (2002) describe problems in preparing performance analyses for application servers due to quickly evolving updates: The survey disclosed that newly introduced product versions have been slower than their predecessors, and new functionalities have caused incompatibilities in the existing application code.

Only after extensive adaptations, which required extremely detailed knowledge of the products concerned, was it possible to restore the desired performance behavior. Regardless of the homogeneity and immaturity problems, current Web applications use many different technical infrastructures to solve given problems.

The range extends from technical open-source frameworks, such as Struts (http://jakarta.apache.org/struts/) and Cocoon (http://xml.apache.org/cocoon/), over application servers like EJB implementations, to portal frameworks like Brazil (http://research.sun.com/brazil/) and Jet Speed (http://jakarta.apache.org/jetspeed/).

In addition, many Web applications use several frameworks concurrently. Lanchorst et al. (2001) categorize and analyze different frameworks. Another aspect that becomes noticeable in the field of WAA is the internationalization of Web applications, requiring the support of different languages, character sets, and representation mechanisms (e.g., representation of Arabic characters from right to left) on the WPA level.

KEYWORD

Multimedia data refers to data that consist of various media types like text, audio, video, and animation.

Many of these aspects are supported by programming languages or operating systems. For example, the Java platform offers internationalization mechanisms, reaching from different character encodings (e.g., ISO-8859-1, UTF-8) to multi-language user interfaces by using so-called "resource bundles."

All these different aspects need to be considered when developing architectures for web applications. In particular, WPAs provide a wide range of functionalities to solve common problems, and they define the context in which web applications may evolve.

Further sections give an overview of common components of WPA and show how these architectures support the development of Web applications.

4.7. DATA-ASPECT ARCHITECTURES

Data can be grouped into either of three architectural categories: (1) structured data of the kind held in databases; (2) documents of the kind used in document management systems; and (3) multimedia data of the kind held in media servers. In this respect, Web applications are normally not limited to one of these data categories; they rather integrate documents, media, and databases. We will have a closer look at these categories in subsections.

4.7.1. Database-Centric Architectures

Several tools and approaches are available to integrate databases into Web applications. These databases are accessed either directly from within Web server extensions (in the case of 2-layer architectures) or over application servers (in the case of n-layer architectures). Since database technologies (and particularly relational databases) are highly mature, they are easy to integrate.

APIs are available for different platforms, e.g., Java database connectivity (JDBC) for Java-based applications or open database connectivity (ODBC) for Microsoft technologies (Saake & Sattler, 2003), to access relational databases. Bongio et al. (2003) describe the design of data-intensive Web applications.

4.7.2. Architectures for Web Document Management

In addition to structured data held in databases and multimedia data held on media servers, the contents of Web applications are often processed in the form of documents. Content management architectures support the integration of documents from different sources, representing a mechanism to integrate these contents into Web applications.

KEYWORD

Content management system (CMS) is computer software used to manage the creation and modification of digital content (content management).

This section discusses important aspects of architectures used to integrate external content. A detailed description of the functionalities and tasks involved in content management systems (CMS), i.e., systems that implement content management architectures, is found in the literature (Jablonski & Meiler, 2002).

A Web server receives a client request and forwards it to a content delivery server. The content delivery server is responsible for distributing – and perhaps caching – the contents. If the requested content is not in the cache, then the request is forwarded to the content management server.

The content can be available directly on that server (in static form as a document or in a content database), or it can be accessed externally. Depending on the type of integration, external content can be retrieved either by accessing external databases (directly or by use of an aggregation service) or from a syndication service. In contrast to accessing a database, syndication services can handle additional functionalities, e.g., automated billing of licensing rights.

One example of a publisher component to prepare static XML documents is the Cocoon 2 open-source framework. Cocoon 2 supports the publication of XML documents on the Web. Its range of applications is primarily the transformation of XML content documents into different output formats.

The underlying processing work is based on a pipeline model, i.e., a request is accepted and forwarded to a generator pre-defined in a configuration file. The XML document is subject to several processing steps within the pipeline to bring it into the desired output format.

All processing steps in the pipeline can access information about the request, e.g., the user agent, to adapt the response to the request (e.g., user interface customization).

The generator is called at the beginning of the process; it is responsible for parsing the XML document. The generator uses the SAX parser to read the XML document and then generates SAX messages called events.

The generator has to forward these events to the pipeline. These SAX events can be used to transform or forward the document. This means that the generator makes data available for processing. The transformer can be compared with an XSL style sheet.

Finally, a serialize is responsible for converting to the desired output format, e.g., HTML or XML, again. A powerful configuration mechanism in the form of an XML configuration file can be used to select and define generator, transformer, and serialized. For example, the configuration routine lets one control the processing pipeline depending on the request and the processing results.

Did you Know?

The framework serves as a blueprint for the basic architecture and basic functionalities for a specific field of application. This means that the architectural knowledge contained in a framework can be fully adopted in the application.

4.7.3. Architectures for Multimedia Data

The ability to handle large data volumes plays a decisive role when designing multimedia content systems. While the data volume is normally not decisive in database-centric Web applications, it considerably influences the architecture and design of multimedia Web applications.

A detailed overview of architectural issues concerning multimedia data in Web applications can also be found in Srinivasan et al. (2001). Basically, multimedia data, i.e., audio and video, can be transmitted over standard Internet protocols like HTTP or FTP, just like any other data used in Web applications.

Many current Web applications use this approach because it has the major benefit that no additional components are needed on the server. However, users often feel its downside in that the media downloads are very slow.

We can use streaming technologies to minimize these waiting times for multimedia content to play out. Streaming in this context means that a client can play out of the audio and/or video a few seconds after it begins receiving the file from a server. This technique avoids downloading the entire file (incurring a potentially long delay) before beginning the payout. The contents have to be transmitted in real-time, which requires a corresponding bandwidth, and low jitter, to ensure continuous play out of the contents. A guaranteed transmission bandwidth is appropriately called quality of service (QOS).

Two protocols are generally used for the streaming of multimedia content. One protocol handles the transmission of multimedia data on the network level. The other protocol controls the presentation flow (e.g., starting and stopping a video) and meta-data transmission.

One good example of a network protocol is the real time protocol (RTP), which collaborates with a control protocol, the Real Time Streaming Protocol (RTSP). In addition to these popular protocols, there are several proprietary products, e.g., progressive networks audio (PNA) and progressive networks metafile (PNM) of Real Networks (http://www.real.com), or the Microsoft Media Server (MMS) protocol.

KEYWORD

Network protocol is an established set of rules that determine how data is transmitted between different devices in the same network.

We can identify two distinct fields of application for multimedia data streaming. First, making existing content available on demand, e.g., video-on-demand, and second, broadcasting live content to many users, e.g., Web casting. Each of these two use cases poses totally different requirements on the network and the hardware and software architectures.

While each user establishes their own connection to the server in an on-demand scenario, causing major bandwidth and server load problems, broadcasting makes especially high demands on the network level. Examples are given by Srinivasan et al. (2001) and Roy et al. (2003).

Ideally, a server used for broadcasting should manage one single media stream, which is simultaneously broadcasted to all users by the network infrastructure (e.g., by routers), as visualized. However, since multicasting is not generally supported on the Internet, the server has to use point-to-point connections, similar to the on-demand scenario, to "simulate" the broadcast functionality.

To keep such systems scalable to the desired number of users, it is often necessary to distribute multimedia data to keep the users' access paths as short as possible. This approach forwards a user's request to the nearest node that holds the required data.

KEYWORD

Spatial distribution is the arrangement of a phenomenon across the Earth's surface and a graphical display of such an arrangement is an important tool in geographical and environmental statistics.

The distribution itself can be based on either a push or a pull mechanism. The push mechanism wouldn't transmit the contents to a local node unless at least one user or a specific number of users requested them. This mechanism is typically used when there is no information about the spatial distribution of the user group.

In contrast, the pull mechanism transmits the contents by a pre-defined distribution plan, which means that the media distribution can be optimized with regard to the transmission medium (e.g., satellite) and the transmission time (e.g., overnight).

Of course, this type of distribution needs to know the local distribution of the user group. Building such a distribution infrastructure is very costly and maintenance-intensive, which is the reason why it is not widely used.

SUMMARY

- **What is Architecture?:** This section of the chapter explains you the Web architecture and its types – developing architecture and categorizing architecture. This chapter has also discussed pervasive web application architecture and Application Scenario.
- **How to Build Web Applications?:** This part summarizes the building of a web application. There are different ways: web page design resources, Web site design resources, Web application design resources, and Principles of Web application design.
- **TCP/IP:** The end of the chapter summarizes about the transmission control protocol (TCP) and Internet Protocol. Layers, the client paradigm, and Specifics of Web Application Architecture have also been explained in this chapter.

Data aspect architectures and their types – database centric architectures, Architecture for Web document management and Architecture for multimedia data summarizes this chapter.

REVIEW QUESTIONS

1. What is architecture? Explain its types.
2. What do you understand by pervasive web application architecture?
3. What are application scenarios?
4. What is transmission control protocol?
5. What is internet protocol?
6. What is a specific of web application architecture?
7. What is data aspect architecture?

MULTIPLE CHOICE QUESTIONS

1. TCP stands for:

a. Transmission control protocol
b. Transparent control protocol
c. Telephone control protocol
d. None

2. Which of the following examples are models of application architecture?

a. Means of assessing components for reuse
b. Design checklist

c. Vocabulary for talking about types of applications
d. All of the above

3. Which of the following are commonly used architectural patterns?
a. Model view controller
b. Layered architecture
c. Client server
d. All of the above

4. Systems that involve interaction with a shared database can be considered as follows:
a. Software based
b. Transaction based
c. Server based
d. Client based

5. Which of the following type describes the application architectures?
a. Transaction processing applications
b. Language processing applications
c. Client management system
d. Both a and b

Answers to Multiple Choice Questions

1. (a) 2. (d) 3. (d) 4. (b) 5. (d)

REFERENCES

1. Kuuskeri, J., (2014). *Engineering Web Applications: Architectural Principles for Web Software.* Academia.edu. academia. Available at: https://www.academia.edu/6105885/Engineering_Web_Applications_Architectural_Principles_for_Web_Software (accessed on 04 March 2023).
2. Madeyski, L., & Stochmialek, M., (2005). Architectural design of modern web applications. www.researchgate.net. *Foundations of Computing and Decision Sciences.* Available at: https://www.researchgate.net/publication/221679095_Architectural_Design_of_Modern_Web_Applications (accessed on 04 March 2023).
3. *Pervasive Web Application Architecture,* (n.d). www.idc-online.com. technical_references. Available at: https://www.idc-online.com/technical_references/pdfs/information_technology/Pervasive_Web_Application_Architecture.pdf (accessed on 04 March 2023).

4. Shklar, L., & Rosen, R., (2003). *Web Application Architecture: Principles, Protocols and Practices*, www.bedford-computing.co.uk. John Wiley & Sons Ltd. Available at: http://bedford-computing.co.uk/learning/wp-content/uploads/2016/07/Web-Application-Architecture-Principles-Protocols-and-Practices.pdf (accessed on 04 March 2023).
5. Shklar, L., & Rosen, R., (2009). *Web Application Architecture Principles, Protocols and Practices*. download.e-bookshelf.de. John Wiley & Sons Ltd. Available at: https://download.e-bookshelf.de/download/0000/5960/33/L-G-0000596033-0002363371.pdf (accessed on 04 March 2023).
6. Shklar, L., & Rosen, R., (2009). *Web Application Architecture: Principles, Protocols and Practices, PDF Drive*. John Wiley & Sons. Available at: https://www.pdfdrive.com/web-application-architecture-principles-protocols-and-practices-e177447614.html (accessed on 04 March 2023).
7. Shklar, L., & Rosen, R., (2009). *Web Application Architecture: Principles, Protocols and Practices*. Wiley.com. John Wiley & Sons Ltd. Available at: https://www.wiley.com/en-ae/Web+ Application+Architecture:+Principles,+Protocols+and+Practices,+2nd+Edition-p-9780470518601 (accessed on 04 March 2023).

CHAPTER 5

WEB BIG DATA AND DATA ANALYTICS

UNIT INTRODUCTION

In the previous unit, we discussed the web application architectures (WAA) under this unit, the meaning of architectures, developing architectures, and categorizing architectures. We discussed the pervasive web application architecture, application scenarios, TCP/IP, and data-aspect architectures we discussed in this chapter.

Now in the present unit, we will extend our discussion on the definition of big data, including with history of big data, and also discuss the analyst perspective on data repositories, characteristics of big data, and types of big data analytics. We will discuss the big data importance and applications of big data analytics we will discuss in this chapter.Data is produced continuously and at an accelerating rate. Mobile devices, social media, and imaging technology used to make medical diagnoses all produce fresh data, which must be kept somewhere for a specific reason.

Devices and sensors automatically generate diagnostic data, which must be saved and processed immediately. It's challenging enough to keep up with this massive inflow of data, but it's much harder to analyze vast amounts of it to find significant patterns and extract usable information, especially when it doesn't follow conventional ideas of data structure. These data deluge difficulties present opportunities to alter business, government, science, and daily life. Several industries have taken the lead in improving their capacity to collect and use data:

- Credit card firms keep track of every transaction their users make, and by applying criteria developed by processing billions of transactions, they can accurately identify fraudulent transactions.
- Mobile phone companies look through customer call histories to determine whether a caller's regular contacts are on a different network. The mobile phone provider can proactively incentivize the subscriber to stay in her contract if the competing network runs an alluring promotion that could lead the user to leave.
- Data is the main product for companies like LinkedIn and Facebook. These businesses' valuations heavily depend on the data they collect and host, which has increasing inherent value as the volume of data increases.

Three factors can best summarize big data features:

- **Huge Volume of Data:** Big data can have billions of rows and millions of columns rather than thousands or millions of rows.
- **Complexity of Data Types and Structures:** Big data reflects the diversity of new data sources, formats, and structures, such as digital traces left on the internet and in other digital repositories for future analysis.
- **Speed of New Data Creation and Growth:** Big data is a term used to describe data that is processed quickly and in close to real time.

Although the volume of Big Data frequently garners the most attention, the diversity and speed of the data typically provide a more accurate description of big data (big data is sometimes described as having 3 Vs: volume, variety, and velocity.

Because of its size or structure, Big Data cannot be effectively evaluated using simply conventional databases or techniques. Big data issues demand new tools and technology to store, manage, and reap the benefits for the business. Large datasets can be created, manipulated, and managed using these new tools and technologies, as well as the storage environments that hold them.

Learning Objectives

Following the completion of the chapter, the students should be able to understand the following:

- Understand what big data is;
- Learn about the arrival of analytics;
- Understand the history of big data;
- Understand the analyst perspective on data repositories;
- Understand big data analytics;
- Understand the characteristics of big data;
- Understand the different types of big data analytics;

- Understand the skills set of data analytics;
- Understand the importance of big data.

Key Terms

- Analytics
- Perspective
- Descriptive
- Diagnostic
- Predictive
- Prescriptive

5.1. WHAT IS BIG DATA?

What precisely is big data? At first look, the phrase appears quite ambiguous, alluding to something substantial and information rich. Although the definition is accurate, it doesn't explain what big data actually is (Figure 5.1).

Figure 5.1. *Big data.*

Source: Image by Flickr.

Big data is sometimes defined as extraordinarily massive data collections that are too big to manage and analyze using conventional data processing techniques. Searching the Web for clues reveals an almost universal definition shared by most individuals pushing the ideology of Big Data, which may be summarized into something like this.

Big data describes a situation in which data sets have gotten so big that traditional information technology (IT) cannot adequately handle the data collection's size or its scale and growth. In other words, the data set has become so enormous that it is challenging to manage and even more challenging to extract value from it. The main challenges are with data collection, storage, searching, sharing, analytics, and visualization.

There is much more to be stated on what Big Data is in reality. The idea has developed to consider both the size of the data set and the procedures involved in utilizing the data. Big Data is now used interchangeably with business terms like business intelligence, analytics, and data mining.

Ironically, big data isn't all that new. Big Data has its origins in the scientific and medical communities, where the intricate analysis of enormous amounts of data has been done for drug development, physics modeling, and other forms of research, all of which involve large data sets, even though massive data sets have only been created in the last two years. However, it is from these very conceptual beginnings that Big Data has evolved.

5.1.1. The Arrival of Analytics

As analytics and research were applied to enormous data sets, scientists came to the notion that more is better—in this case, more data, more analysis, and more results. Researchers began integrating related data sets, unstructured data, archive data, and real-time data into the procedure, giving rise to what is now known as big data.

In the business world, Big Data is all about the opportunity. According to IBM, we generate 2.5 quintillion (2.5–3x10^{18}) bytes of data daily, meaning that 90% of the data today was produced in the previous two years. These data originate from various sources, including online posts to social media sites, digital images and videos posted online, transaction records of transactions made online, and cell phone GPS signals, to mention a few.

TIPS

Microsoft excel software is used to create forms, power pivot, pivot tables, dashboards etc.

In addition to the more significant fact that all of this data has intrinsic value that can be extrapolated through analytics, algorithms, and other techniques, that serves as the impetus for big data. Big Data has already proved its importance and value in several areas.

Organizations like the National Oceanic and Atmospheric Administration (NOAA), the National Aeronautics and Space Administration (NASA), several pharmaceutical companies, and numerous energy companies have accumulated enormous amounts of data and now use Big Data technologies regularly to extract value from them.

NASA uses big data techniques for aeronautical and other research, while NOAA employs them to support climate, ecological, weather, and commercial research. Companies in the pharmaceutical and energy sectors have used big data for more practical outcomes like geophysical analysis and drug testing.

Big data tools have been utilized for text analysis and web mining by The New York Times, while The Walt Disney Company employs them to correlate and comprehend consumer behavior across all of its retail locations, theme parks, and online businesses.

Today's enterprises use big data for additional purposes: To comply with government rules, large firms increasingly need to keep enormous amounts of structured and unstructured data, including employee tweets, supplier records, data warehouse transaction information, and regulatory filings.

Recent court decisions that have pushed businesses to retain significant amounts of paperwork, electronic mail, and other communications like instant messaging and phone calls from Internet service providers that may be needed for e-discovery in the event of litigation have increased the need for this even more.

KEYWORD

Electronic mail is the exchange of computer-stored messages from one user to one or more recipients via the internet.

5.2. THE HISTORY OF BIG DATA

Although the idea of big data is relatively new, the earliest data centers and the creation of relational databases can be found in the 1960s and 1970s, when the world of data was just beginning. Around 2005, people discovered just how much data consumers generated through Facebook, YouTube, and other online services.

The same year saw the development of Hadoop, an open-source framework designed primarily to store and process large data collections. NoSQL also began to gain popularity during this time. The emergence of open-source frameworks like Hadoop (and, more recently, Spark) was crucial for expanding big data since they make enormous data more manageable and more affordable to store.

Since then, the amount of big data has exponentially increased; users are still producing large volumes of data, but not just humans. The Internet of Things (IoT) has enabled more products and gadgets to connect to the Internet, collecting information on consumer usage trends and product performance.

The development of machine learning has led to the creation of even more data. Despite how far big data has come, its value is still in its infancy. Big data possibilities have been further increased by cloud computing. Developers may easily spin up ad hoc clusters in the cloud to test a subset of data since it has true elastic scalability.

Benefits of big data and data analytics:

- Big data enables you to obtain more comprehensive answers since it gives you access to more data;
- More thorough responses increase data confidence, which calls for a fundamentally different strategy for problem-solving.

5.3. BIG DATA ANALYTICS

Data is the most effective resource in the world for giving countries, organizations, and corporations a competitive edge. There are reportedly 2.5 quintillion bytes of data produced per day from various sources (Figure 5.2):

Figure 5.2. *Big data analytics.*

Source: Image by Flickr.

- **Data:** Depending on the interests of the people involved, the word "data" is defined from a variety of perspectives. For instance, data is the unprocessed information from various sources used by researchers to produce the final product.

The quantities, characters, or symbols that a computer performs operations on and which may be saved and transferred as electrical signals and recorded on magnetic, optical, or mechanical storage media are referred to as data.

The terms bit, byte, kilobyte, megabyte, gigabyte, etc., are used to define data in computer science and are frequently used to differentiate binary machines – readable information derived from human-readable textual information.

For instance, some programs distinguish between data files (files containing binary data) and text files (files that contain ASCII1 data). We define data in this sense as anything that uses bits or bytes from a computer's hard disc or memory. Data has grown to be so potent that many new disciplines, like database management systems (DBMS), data science, data analytics, and others, have been born from it.

Many data-related concepts have evolved as a result of data. Numerous words have been used to describe data over the years as technology has changed and advanced.

Big data refers to a new type of data that has emerged as a result of how we utilize and analyze data, data structure, large volumes, etc., words like "data integrity" and "data mining" are still used frequently today. Definitions of data assist us in comprehending data and its use in IT and business analysis.

KEYWORD

Data processing system is a combination of machines, people, and processes that for a set of inputs produces a defined set of outputs.

- **Big Data:** A massive volume of both structured and unstructured data that is so large it is difficult to process using traditional database and software techniques. In most enterprise scenarios, the volume of data is too big, it moves too fast, or it exceeds the current processing capacity.

Big data has the potential to help companies improve operations and make faster, more intelligent decisions. The data is collected from several sources, including emails, mobile devices, applications, databases, servers, and other means.

When captured, formatted, manipulated, stored, and then analyzed, this data can help a company gain useful insight to increase revenues, get or retain customers and improve operations. Big Data is a field of study that focuses on extracting and analyzing information that is too complex to be dealt with by traditional data processing systems.

It deals with the massive volume of both structured and programmed data and unstructured data or non-programmed data that is too large to process using traditional software. Big Data has the potential to help companies improve operations and make faster, more intelligent decisions.

The data is collected from a few sources, including emails, mobile devices, applications, databases, servers, and other means (Grimes, 2019). When captured, formatted, manipulated, stored, and then analyzed, this data can help a company gain useful insight to increase revenues, get or retain customers and improve operations.

5.3.1. Characteristics of Big Data

Big data can be well understood by its characteristics. Big data is characterized by 6Vs shown in the following:

- **Volume:** The name Big Data itself is related to its enormous size. Data size plays a crucial role in determining its value out of data. Also, whether data can be considered Big Data or not depends on the volume of data. Hence, 'Volume' is one characteristic that needs to be considered while dealing with Big Data. As we know, the volume of data is measured by bit, bite, kilobyte, megabyte, gigabyte, terabyte, petabyte, exabyte, etc.
- **Variety:** The next aspect of Big Data is its variety. Variety refers to heterogeneous sources and the nature of data, both structured and unstructured. In earlier days, spreadsheets and databases were the only data sources considered by most applications.

Nowadays, data in the form of emails, photos, videos, monitoring devices, PDFs, audio, etc., are also being considered in the analysis applications. Data also can be grouped in terms of structure.

Some data can be classified as structured data, and some as unstructured others may fall into the spectrum called semi-structured and quasi-structured. This variety of unstructured data poses certain storage, mining, and analysis issues.

KEYWORD

Structured data is data that has been organized into a formatted repository, typically a database.

Structured data refers to any data that resides in a fixed field within a record or file. This includes data contained in relational databases and spreadsheets. Structured data first depends on creating a data model – a model of the types of business data that will be recorded and how they will be stored, processed, and accessed.

This includes defining what fields of data will be stored and how that data will be stored: data type (numeric, currency, alphabetic, name, date, address) and any restrictions on the data input (number of characters; restricted to certain terms such as Mr., Ms, or Dr.; M or F, etc.

Structured data has the advantage of being easily entered, stored, queried, and analyzed. At one time, because of the high cost and performance limitations of storage, memory, and processing, relational databases and spreadsheets using structured data were the only way to manage data effectively.

Anything that couldn't fit into a tightly organized structure would have to be stored on paper in a filing cabinet. Unstructured Data refers to any data not residing in a traditional row-column database. As you might expect, it's the opposite of structured data.

Unstructured data files often include text and multimedia content. Examples include e-mail messages, word processing documents, videos, photos, audio files, presentations, webpages, and many other kinds of business documents.

Note that while these sorts of files may have an internal structure, they are still considered "unstructured" because the data they contain doesn't fit neatly in a database. Experts estimate that 80% to 90% of the data in any organization is unstructured.

And the amount of unstructured data in enterprises is growing significantly — often, many times faster than structured databases are growing. Semi-structured Data: In this form of data, the schema is not properly defined, i.e., both forms of data are present.

KEYWORD

Unstructured data is information that is not arranged according to a preset data model or schema, and therefore cannot be stored in a traditional relational database or RDBMS.

So, semi-structured data has a structured form, but it isn't defined, e.g., JSON, XML, CSV, TSV, and email.

The unstructured web application data contains transaction history files, log files, etc. OLTP systems (Online Transaction Processing) are built to work with structured data, and the data is stored in relations, i.e., tables.

Quasi structured data format consists of textual data with inconsistent data formats that can be formatted with effort and time and with the help of several tools. For example, web server logs, i.e., a log file automatically created and maintained by some server containing a list of activities.

- **Velocity:** The term "velocity" refers to the speed of the generation of data. The speed of data generation and accumulation also plays a role in determining whether the data is classified as big data or small data.

With the development of technology, the need for velocity has become an essential element without which new technologies nowadays cannot work effectively—Twitter, Facebook, instant messages, Google searches, e-mails, new data creation, etc.

At first, mainframes were used, wherein fewer people used computers. Then came the client/server model, and more and more computers evolved. After this, web applications came into the picture and increased over the internet.

Then, everyone began using these applications. These applications were then used by more and more devices, such as mobiles, as they were very easy to access. Hence, a lot of data! As it is clear from the image, every 60 seconds, so much of the data is generated. How fast the data is generated and processed to meet the demands determines the real potential of the data. Big Data Velocity deals with the speed at which data flows in from sources like business processes, application logs, networks, social media sites, sensors, Mobile devices, etc. The flow of data is massive and continuous.

- **Variability:** This refers to the inconsistency of data that can be shown by the data at times, thus hampering the process of handling and managing the data effectively. Data loads become challenging to maintain, especially with increased social media usage, which generally causes peak data loads with certain events occurring.
- **Value Chain:** It refers to the process of making the big data more valuable that adds value through the chain of extraction, manipulation, use, and implementation of big data. The process that will extract, clean and process data has lots of value addition.

At the outset, one needs to mine the data, i.e., a process to turn raw data into useful data. Then, an analysis is done on the data you have cleaned or retrieved from the raw data. Afterward, one needs to make sure whatever analysis they do, has benefits business, such as in finding out insights, results, etc., which were not possible earlier.

One needs to make sure that whatever raw data you are given, they have cleaned it to be used for deriving business insights. After data is cleaned, a challenge pops up, i.e., while dumping a huge amount of data, some packages might have lost.

- **Veracity:** Data quality is unreliable as data comes from various uncontrolled sources. The actual and potential value of Big Data is virtually worthless if the data is not accurate.

This is particularly true in programs that involve automated decision-making or feeding the data into an unsupervised machine learning algorithm. The results of such programs are only as good as the data they are working with.

If you have customer behavior data and want to predict the purchase intent of the customer. The customer data you have in log files in various formats and systems are incomplete or surrounded by noise and errors that are to be copied, translated, and unified. Data analysts must ensure that they are cleaned up before they start playing with data. Sometimes the data analyst's

Remember

A sentiment analysis system for text analysis combines natural language processing and machine learning techniques to assign weighted sentiment scores to the entities, topics, themes and categories within a sentence or phrase.

job revolves so much around cleaning up messy data that he is more of a 'data janitor' than a data scientist or data analyst.

What is crucial to understanding big data is its messy, noisy nature and the amount of work that goes into producing an accurate dataset before analysis can even begin.

5.4. TYPES OF BIG DATA ANALYTICS

There are four different types of big data analytics. These are descriptive, diagnostic, predictive, and prescriptive data analytics (Figure 5.3). Big data analytics is a broad field, so each type of analytics has individual goals and objectives in business applications:

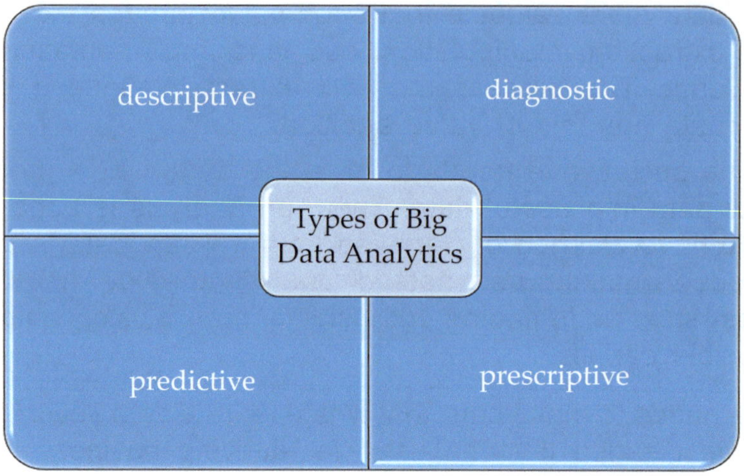

Figure 5.3. *Types of big data analytics.*

5.4.1. Descriptive Data Analytics

Does descriptive data analysis deal with revealing "what happened"? It provides large data sets in a digestible and coherent form. This type of data analysis is more data analysis and less data analytics. It needs the collection of relevant past data, processing of the data, and presenting it in visual form.

It represents what happened in the past. This is the basic type of analysis that provides a backbone for other data analytics. It answers the questions like: 'What is going on'? 'How is it going on'? Examples of descriptive analysis are key performance indicators (KPI) to track the success and failure of indicators.

Return on investment (ROI) which fined the return on investment after a given period. Metrics on specialized indicators to find the successful performance of industries. Descriptive Data analysis tools are Microsoft Excel, statistical package for social sciences (SPSS), data envelopment analysis (DEI), interactive data Extraction and Analysis (IDEA), Stata, R, etc.

5.4.2. Diagnostic Analytics

Diagnostic analytics deal with the "why happened" question. It provides a deeper analysis from descriptive analytics. It identifies the cause and reaction of a situation. This type of data analytics needs information from descriptive analytics and further investigates the information for a better understanding of why a situation gets better or worse.

TIPS

Researchers started to incorporate related data sets, unstructured data, archival data, and real-time data into the process, which in turn gave birth to what we now call big data.

Example: Selecting the best candidate based on quality, competence, and tenure. Diagnostic analytics requires three steps to conduct any study. The first one is anomaly detection. Anomaly detection means finding any interruption or unexpected changes in an activity—for example, the rising demand for salt.

The second step is the investigation of anomalies. It is the process of finding how an interruption or unexpected cause happened. Similar data to the anomaly is identified in this stage. The sources of data and finding patterns of those data are identified (Grover & Kar, 2017).

For example, increased onion prices and shortage of onion in the warehouse may cause unexpected demand for salt in the market. The third and final step is the determination of a casual relationship. In this stage, the relationship and trends are identified for anomalies.

To identify the cause and reaction, statistical analysis like probability analysis, time series analysis, or regression analysis can be applied. Diagnostic analytics Data analysis tools are Microsoft Excel, statistical package for social sciences (SPSS), DEI, IDEA, Stata, R, etc.

5.4.3. Predictive Analytics

Predictive analytics deals with the question of "what will happen?" question. It identifies the future trends and possible outcomes of a situation. This type of analytics needs historical data to find future occurrences.

Neural networks, decision trees, regression analysis, etc., are used for predictive analysis (Amado, 2018). Example: Prediction of result, probabilities of a certain scenario, possible outcome of diseases, market trend in the stock exchange and future trends on consumer behavior, determine marketing mix, etc.

Data analysis tools are Microsoft Excel (higher level) like regression, forecasting, solver, et., statistical package for social sciences (SPSS), IDEA, Stata, R, ithnk, Arena, Vensim, etc.

5.4.4. Prescriptive Analytics

Remember

The data gathered from devices helps organizations in determining when and how intense maintenance is required by a specific machine.

Prescriptive Analytics deals with the question of "what should be done?" question. It identifies the possible solutions for problems in predictive analysis (Lepenioti et al., 2019). This type of analysis needs data from predictive analysis to provide possible courses of action for a given scenario.

For example, what product price maximizes profit? How can an organization choose projects that maximize corporate objectives subject to limited resources? What minimizes operating costs? Where should warehouses be located to minimize the distance that shipments must travel? How should workers be assigned to jobs to make both the bosses and employees happy?

Data analysis tools are Microsoft Excel (higher level) like regression, forecasting, solver, etc., statistical package for social sciences (SPSS), IDEA, Stata, R, ithnk, Arena, Vensim, etc.

5.4.5. Other Types of Big Data Analytics

Other types of analytics are based on the objectives and types of data analyzed to get specific insights into the business. These are text analytics, sentiment analytics, web analytics, etc.

- **Text Analytics:** It is the process of converting unstructured data into meaningful text data. It uses linguistic, statistical, and machine learning techniques. Text analytics measures customer opinion, product review, feedback, and entity modeling to enhance decision making. It requires tagging, clustering, pattern recognition, visualization, etc., to extract meaningful text data from unstructured data (Clarabridge, 2019).
- **Sentiment Analytics:** It determines whether a piece

of writing is positive, negative, or neutral. A sentiment analysis system for text analysis combines natural language processing and machine learning techniques to assign weighted sentiment scores to the entities, topics, themes, and categories within a sentence or phrase.

It helps data analysts within large enterprises gauge public opinion, conduct nuanced market research, monitor brand and product reputation, and understand customer experiences (Towards Data Science, 2019).

- **Web Analytics:** It is the process of analyzing the behavior of visitors to a Web site (Sterne, 2002). Web analytics enables a business to attract more visitors, retain or attract new customers for goods or services, or increase the dollar volume each customer spends.

It addresses the questions about the navigation tour and the intention of the visitors and traffics on the site, the hit generated, observation, recommendations made, etc.

KEYWORD

Sentiment analysis is an approach to natural language processing (NLP) that identifies the emotional tone behind a body of text.

5.5. SKILLS SET OF A DATA ANALYST

A data analyst is a person who uses data analysis of analytics software to convert the raw data into meaningful insight so that effective decisions can be made (Dataquest, 2019). As stated by some scholars, data analysts combine a specific set of skills.

Data quest (2019) identified the skill set as follows:

- **Computing Skill:** Use advanced computerized models to extract the data needed;
- **Editing Skill:** Remove corrupted data;
- **Validation Skill:** Perform initial analysis to assess the quality of the data;
- **Analysis Skill:** Perform further analysis to determine the meaning of the data;
- **Justification Skill:** Perform a final analysis to provide additional data screening;
- **Reporting Skill:** Prepare reports based on analysis and presentation to management.

The skills needed to be a data analyst also has been prescribed by Brink& Stoel (2019) as high-level mathematical ability, the ability to analyze, model, and interpret data, high-level mathematical ability, problem-solving skills, a methodical and logical approach, the ability to plan work and meet deadlines, accuracy, and attention to detail, interpersonal skills.

The skill set for big data analytics is multidisciplinary. It also includes Programming skills. While traditional data analysts might be able to get away without being full-fledged programmers, a big data analyst needs to be very comfortable with coding.

KEYWORD

Python is a high-level, general-purpose programming language.

One of the main reasons for this requirement is that big data is still evolving. Not many standard processes are set around the large complex datasets a big data analyst must handle. A lot of customization is required daily to deal with unstructured data.

Data scientist needs some specific computer languages such as R, Python, Java, C++, Ruby, SQL, Hive, SAS, SPSS, MATLAB, Weka, Julia, and Scala. At the minimum one needs to know R, Python, and Java. While working one may end up using various tools.

It requires:

- **Data Warehousing Knowledge:** Experience with relational and non-relational database systems is a must. Examples of the relational database include – MySQL, Oracle, and DB2. Examples of the non-relational database include – NoSQL, HBase, HDFS, MongoDB, CouchDB, Cassandra, Teradata, etc. It needs Computational skills.
- **Computational Frameworks:** A good understanding and familiarity with frameworks such as Apache Spark, Apache Storm, Apache Samza, Apache Flink, and the classic MapReduce and Hadoop. These technologies help big data processing, which can be streamed to a great extent.
- **Quantitative Aptitude and Statistical Skills are Needed as well:** While the processing of big data requires great use of technology, fundamental to any analysis of data is good knowledge of Statistics and linear algebra.

Statistics is a basic building block of data science, and understanding core concepts like summary statistics, probability distribution, random variables, and Hypothesis testing framework is important if you are a data scientist of any genre.

Business knowledge is important to conduct good analytics. To keep the analysis focused, validate, sort, relate, and evaluate the data, the most critical skill of a big data scientist is to have a good knowledge of the domain one is working on. In fact, big data analysts are so much in demand because it's very rare to find resources that have a thorough understanding of technical aspects, statistics, and business.

TIPS

Unstructured data refers to any data that doesn't reside in a traditional row-column database.

To keep the analysis focused, to validate, sort, relate, evaluate the data, the most critical skill of a big data scientist is to have a good knowledge of the domain one is working on.

In fact, the reason big data analysts are so much in demand is that it's very rare to find resources that have a thorough understanding of technical aspects, statistics, and business. There are analysts good in business and statistics but not in programming.

There are expert programmers without the know-how of how to put the programs in the context of the business goal. Lastly, a good hold on machine learning is highly beneficial as it helps in managing complex data structures and learning patterns that are too difficult to handle using traditional data analytics.

5.5.1. Software Needed for Data Analytics

Data analytics is done with the help of machine learning and algorithm. So, the software is needed to analyze data in data analytics (Zhang & Xie, 2019). The software that is needed in data analytics is of various types. Microsoft Excel software is used to create forms, power pivots, pivot tables, dashboards, etc., to analyze and report data.

It has lots of features, including reporting, describing, diagnosing, analyzing, forecasting, making queries, reengineering and restructuring, filtering, formatting, looking up, visualizing, modeling, etc. Business Intelligent tools or software is used for data cleaning, processing, modeling, and visualizing data.

Examples are Tableau, Power BI, Fine Report software, etc. This software's features include Ranking Reports, What-If Analysis, Executive Dashboards, Interactive Reports, Geospatial Mapping, Operational Reports, Pivot Tables, and Ad-Hoc Reports. R, Python, Stata, SPSS Amos, etc., are used to code anything one wants to decide on (Rprojectorg, 2019).

Features are Data handling and storage facility, Calculations on arrays, matrices, Collection of big data tools for data analysis, Graphical facilities for data analysis. Discover insights and solve problems faster by analyzing structured and unstructured data, use an intuitive interface for everyone to learn, cloud, and hybrid deployment options, quickly choose the best performing algorithm based on model performance, etc.

Simulation software models' realistic scenarios so that predictive results can be found visually. Simulation software is iThink, Arena, Vensim Simul, etc. Features of this software generally include Animation, Statistical feature, documentation, output report and plots, visualization, forecasting, scenario analysis, etc. Other tools are sisense, looker, periscope data, zoho analytics, yellowfin, domo, qlik sense, goodData, brist, IBM analytics, IBM Cognos, IBM Waston, Matlab, Minilab, Google analytics, stata, apache Hadoop, apache spark, SAP business intelligence platform, etc. (Finance Online, 2019).

KEYWORD

Hadoop clusters are composed of a network of master and worker nodes that orchestrate and execute the various jobs across the Hadoop distributed file system.

5.5.2. Big Data Importance

The amount of data is less important if a company does not utilize it. Every company uses data in its own way. The more efficiently a company uses its data, the more potential it has to grow. The importance of big data is related to its usefulness of data.

The importance of big data is stated from many angles. Perhaps the most important factor is Cost Savings. Big Data analytics tools like Hadoop and Cloud-Based Analytics can bring cost advantages to businesses when large amounts of data are to be stored, and parallelly processed, multiple reports are generated, multi-vendors are supported, and multi-stakeholders are benefited.

Time Reduction is another benefit for which big data analytics are important. The high speed of tools like Hadoop and in-memory analytics can easily identify new sources of data, which helps businesses analyze data immediately and make quick decisions based on the learnings.

There are numerous opportunities for cost and time reduction using big data. Big data technologies such as Hadoop clusters are emerging as significantly low-cost options compared to traditional databases. It can play a role in real-time decisions regarding promoting offers and services to customers based on their current locations ((Davenport & Dyché, 2013).

It helps to understand the market conditions: By analyzing big data, one can get a better understanding of current market conditions. For example, by analyzing customers' purchasing behaviors, a company can find out the products that are sold the most and produce products according to this trend.

Big data analytics keeps a company ahead of its competitors. Control of online reputation is another importance of big data analytics through sentiment analytics. Therefore, you can get feedback about who is saying what about company.

If one wants to monitor and improve the online presence of business, then, big data tools can help in all this. It is so significant in Boosting Customer Acquisition and Retention. The customer is the most important asset any business depends on.

No single business can claim success without first having to establish a solid customer base. However, even with a customer base, a business cannot afford to disregard the high competition it faces. If a business is slow to learn what customers are looking for, then it is very easy to begin offering poor quality products.

In the end, loss of clientele will result, and this creates an adverse overall effect on business success. The use of big data allows businesses to observe various customer related patterns and trends. Observing customer behavior is important to trigger loyalty.

Did you Know?

Actual and potential value of Big Data is virtually worthless if the data is not accurate. This is particularly true in programs that involve automated decision-making or feeding the data into an unsupervised machine learning algorithm.

5.6. APPLICATIONS OF BIG DATA ANALYTICS

Big data analytics are used in almost all industries, organizations, and nations. Big data analytics are significantly being applied in manufacturing companies. The exact location of the product can be tracked by big data analytics.

The focus market identifies customer needs. Big data helps to predict the need of customers. This forecasting can be done when companies refer to their supply chain and can help an organization in improving its profitability and workforce (Zhang, 2017).

Manufacturing organizations need to maintain machinery. The machinery needs to be upgraded to run efficiently. Sensor machines can collect information easily. The data gathered from devices helps organizations determine when and how intensely a specific machine requires maintenance.

Big data analytics can help manufacturers keep track of their machines by continually analyzing and focusing on improving the efficiency of devices. Everyday activities are needed to be monitored in any organization.

Big data collects information from every corner of the organization, thus providing valuable insights into day-to-day business operations. The sources of big data are operational machines, databases keeping a log of the number of units produced, and employee records.

This information can help companies in making decisions related to making changes that can be profitable for the organizations. The Health Care organizations like hospitals, clinics, etc., apply big data analytics successfully in their operations.

Big data analytics are applied for diagnostic purposes through data mining and analysis to identify the causes of illness. Predictive and data analytics of genetic, lifestyle, and social circumstances are used to prevent disease.

KEYWORD

Banking is an industry that handles cash, credit, and other financial transactions for individual consumers and businesses alike.

Leveraging aggregate data to drive hyper-personalized care, called precision medicine, is another application of big data analytics. Data-driven medical and pharmacological research to cure disease and discover new treatments and medicine, etc., are the very important outcome of big data analytics in healthcare industries.

It allows the harnessing of big data to spot medication errors and flag potential adverse reactions. Identification of value that drives better potential outcomes for long-term savings can be achieved through health data analytics.

It helps to identify disease trends and health strategies based on demographic, geographic, and socioeconomic factors called population health (Catalyst, 2019)—big data analytics in finance and the banking industry for many practical causes.

Such analytics allows the institution to develop meaningful customer insight. Banks and financial service rendering companies follow their customers' behavior patterns in almost all their banking activities. Big data provides accurate and real-time information about customers.

Customer service in finance, banking, and insurance organizations using big data analytics has become a successful instance. Customer's historical data, current web data, etc., are used to identify customer issues proactively and resolve them even before the customer complains through predictive analytics, analyzing customers' geographical data to help banks optimize ATM locations, for example. The banks are gathering customer experiences through big data analytics to customize websites in real-time. This gives customers a real and pleasant experience. Banks can use analytics to send real-time messages or any communications regarding an account's predictive and prescriptive status using what if scenarios.

With big data analytics, banks can be proactive in enhancing customer service. Big data analytics is used for boosting sales revenues. Big data analytics can accurately access customers' needs, and banks can promote the right types of solutions.

For example, customers' house finance on web sites is most likely in need of a housing loan which can be identified by big data analytics. Fraud detection is a major contribution of big data analytics. It can detect fraud in real-time and prevent it effectively.

Data from third parties and banking networks holds valuable information about customer interactions. Study and analysis of big data can help detect the misuse of credit cards, debit cards, venture credit hazard treatment, business clarity, customer statistics alteration, money laundering, risk mitigation, etc.

KEYWORD

Fraud detection is a set of processes and analyses that allow businesses to identify and prevent unauthorized financial activity.

Government industries are using big data analytics for many purposes. Big data analytics in government has local, national, and international impacts. The government needs to deal with lots of information to make decisions for millions of people.

For example, they need to keep track of various records and databases regarding the citizens, birth, death, TIN, etc. The proper study and analysis of this data help Governments in endless ways, which is possible with big data.

Big data analytics in the insurance industry are being applied effectively. The insurance industry holds importance not only for individuals but also for business companies. Insurance holds a significant place because it supports people during times of uncertainty.

The data collected from these sources are of varying formats and change at tremendous speeds. It uses such analytics for collecting information. As big data refers to gathering data from disparate sources, this feature creates a crucial use case for the insurance industry to pounce on.

Example: When a customer needs driving insurance, the companies can obtain information by big data from which they can calculate the safety levels for driving in the buyer's vicinity and his past driving records.

Based on this, they can also effectively calculate the cost of car insurance. Gaining customer insight is another predominant application of big data in insurance companies. Determining customer experience and making customers the center of a company's attraction is of prime importance to organizations. Those can be identified with big data.

Insurance frauds are a common incidence. Big data use case for fraud detection and reduction in a highly effective manner. Threat mapping is done through big data analytics. When an insurance agent sells insurance, they want to be aware of all the possibilities of things going unfavorably with their customer, making them file a claim.

KEYWORD

Social media is a computer technology that lets people share ideas, opinions, and information through online networks and communities.

Those can be identified with big data. The application of big data in social media perhaps is the best use in the history of big data analytics. In the current scenario, social media is considered the largest data generator.

The stats have shown that around 500+ terabytes of new data get generated into social media databases every day, particularly in the case of Facebook. The data generated mainly consist of videos, photos, message exchanges, etc.

A single activity on any social media site generates a lot of data which is again stored and gets processed whenever required. Since the data stored is in terabytes, it would take a lot of time to process if our legacy systems do it.

Big Data is a solution to this problem. Arguably the world's most popular social media network, with more than 2 billion monthly active users worldwide, Facebook stores enormous amounts of user data, making it a massive data wonderland.

It's estimated that more than 169 million Facebook users will be in the United States alone by 2018. Facebook is the world's fifth most valuable public company, with a market value of approximately $321 billion.

5.7. ANALYST PERSPECTIVE ON DATA REPOSITORIES

With the advent of spreadsheets, business users could easily apply straightforward logic to data that was organized into rows and columns and produce their own analysis of business issues.

Spreadsheets can be made without database administrator training: They can be configured to carry out various tasks swiftly and independently from information technology (IT) teams.

Spreadsheets can be shared easily, and the end user can change the logic used. However, its widespread use may lead to "many interpretations of the truth." In other words, verifying if a specific user has the most up-to-date data and logic in a spreadsheet can be difficult.

Moreover, the information and logic contained in the spreadsheet may also be lost if a laptop is lost or a file is corrupted. This is a persistent problem because spreadsheet programs such as Microsoft Excel are still widely used on computers worldwide.

The necessity to centralize the data is more important than ever due to the rise in data islands (also known as spread marts). As data needs increased, more scalable data warehousing options also increased. These technologies made it possible to handle data centrally, bringing with them features like security, failover, and a single repository where users could rely on having an "official" source of data for financial reporting or other mission-critical operations.

Additionally, this structure allowed for the development of 81 analytical tools and OLAP cubes, which provided easy access to a number of dimensions in an RD8MS. Advanced features made it possible to use in-depth analytical methods like regressions and neural networks.

Enterprise data warehouses (EDWs) are essential for reporting and 81 duties and address many of the issues that the widespread usage of spreadsheets brings about, such as the difficulty of determining which of several spreadsheet versions is the most accurate.

EDWs, together with a robust 81 strategy, give direct data feeds from centralized, controlled, backed up, and secured sources. Despite their advantages, EDWs and 81 tend to limit the flexibility required for thorough or exploratory data processing.

With the EDW model, database administrators (D8As) and IT departments manage and oversee data, while data analysts must rely on IT to access and update the data schemas. Longer lead times for analysts to receive data result from this; most of the time is spent waiting for approvals rather than beginning productive work.

KEYWORD

Information technology (IT) is the use of any computers, storage, networking and other physical devices, infrastructure and processes to create, process, store, secure and exchange all forms of electronic data.

Additionally, the EDW guidelines frequently prevent analysts from creating datasets. Consequently, it is typical for new systems to emerge that are locally administered by power users and include crucial data for creating analytic data sets.

Because these data sources, unlike an EDW, are not maintained, secured, or backed up, IT organizations often detest the existence of data sources outside their control. Analysts can use EDW and 81 to address data availability and accuracy issues.

KEYWORD

Database is an organized collection of structured information, or data, typically stored electronically in a computer system.

However, EDW and 81 provide fresh issues with agility and flexibility that weren't as prominent while working with spreadsheets. The analytical sandbox, which tries to overcome the contradiction for analysts and data scientists with EDW and more formally governed business data, is a solution to this issue.

In this model, the IT department may still maintain the analytic sandboxes, but they will be specifically created to enable robust analytics while being centrally controlled and guarded. These "workspaces," often known as "sandboxes," are intended to let teams study a variety of datasets under restricted conditions; they are not typically utilized for enterprise-level financial reporting or sales dashboards.

Analytical sandboxes frequently provide high-performance computing employing in-database processing, where the analyzes occur within the database. The theory is that running the analytics within the database itself will result in better performance than bringing the data to an external analytical tool.

In-database analytics, as described in "Advanced Analytics – Technology and Tools: In-Database Analytics," establishes connections to multiple data sources within an organization and saves time by eliminating the need to generate these data feeds one at a time.

In-database processing for deep analytics enables faster turnaround time for designing and executing new analytic models while decreasing, though not completely eliminating, the cost associated with data stored on local "shadow" file systems.

Additionally, analytic sandboxes can store a wider variety of data than the normal structured data in the EDW, such as raw data, textual data, and other types of unstructured data, without interfering with crucial production databases. Big Data Analytics initiatives should take a number of factors into account to make sure the strategy matches the targeted objectives. Because of the properties of big data, these initiatives are well suited for supporting high-value, strategic decisions that require complicated processing.

Due to the abundance of data and its complexity, the analytical procedures utilized in this situation must be iterative and flexible. Rapid and complicated analysis demands high-capacity network connections, as well as taking into account the allowable level of delay.

For instance, creating a real-time product recommender for a website places more demands on the system than creating a near real-time recommender, which may still deliver adequate performance but has a little bit more latency and may be less expensive to implement.

KEYWORD

Strategic decisions is the decisions that look after the environment in which the operation of a firm takes place, the total resources, and the people who developed the company.

SUMMARY

- **What is Big Data?:** This part of the chapter explains the big data, its arrival, history, and its characteristics. The analyst perspective on data repositories has also been explained in this chapter.
- **Types of Big Data Analytics:** The different types of big data Analytics have been discussed under this section. They are – descriptive analytics, diagnostic analytics, predictive analytics, and prescriptive analytics, etc. Skills set of a data analytics, Software needed for Data analytics.
- **Importance of Big Data:** The end of the chapter discusses the importance of Big Data and applications of Big data.

REVIEW QUESTIONS

1. What is Big Data?
2. Explain the history of Big Data?
3. What is Big Data Analytics?
4. What are the characteristics of Big Data?
5. What are the different types of Big Data Analytics?
6. What is the Difference between Descriptive and Diagnostic Analytics?
7. What is Prescriptive Analytics?
8. What is the importance of Big Data?

MULTIPLE CHOICE QUESTIONS

1. What are the different features of Big Data Analytics?

a. Open source
b. Scalability
c. Data recovery
d. All of the above

2. What are the main components of Big Data?

a. MapReduce
b. HDFS
c. YARN
d. All of the above

3. Data Analysis uses _________ to get insights from data.

a. Statistical figures

b. Numerical aspects

c. Statistical methods

d. None

4. The process of quantifying data is referred to as:

a. Decoding

b. Structure

c. Enumeration

d. Coding

5. Data Analysis is a process of:

a. Inspecting data

b. Data cleaning

c. Transforming of data

d. All of the above

Answers to Multiple Choice Questions

1. (d) 2. (d) 3. (c) 4. (c) 5. (d)

REFERENCES

1. *Big-Data-Analytics,* (2021). mu.ac.in. wp-content. Available at: https://mu.ac.in/wp-content/uploads/2021/01/BIG-DATA-ANALYTICS.pdf (accessed on 04 March 2023).
2. *Data Science & Big Data Analytics: Discovering, Analyzing, Visualizing and Presenting Data,* (2015). www.csis.pace.edu. John Wiley & Sons, Inc. Available at: http://csis.pace.edu/ctappert/cs816-19fall/books/2015DataScience&BigDataAnalytics.pdf (accessed on 04 March 2023).
3. *Digital Notes on Big Data Analytics,* (2020). www.mrcet.com. Malla Reddy College of Engineering & Technology. Available at: https://mrcet.com/downloads/digital_notes/IT/(R17A0528)%20BIG%20DATA%20ANALYTICS.pdf (accessed on 04 March 2023).
4. Mia, D. M. A. H., (2020). *Big Data Analytics – Welcome to ICMAB*. www.icmab.org.bd. The cost and management. Available at: https://www.icmab.org.bd/wp-content/uploads/2020/03/3.Big-Data.pdf (accessed on 04 March 2023).
5. Mitchell, I., et al., (2012). *Big Data the definitive Guide to the Revolution in Business Analytics*. www.fujitsu.com. Fujitsu Services Ltd. Available at: https://www.fujitsu.com/rs/Images/WhiteBookofBigData.pdf (accessed on 04 March 2023).

6. Riahi, Y., & Riahi, S., (2018). Big data and big data analytics: Concepts, types and technologies. *International Journal of Research and Engineering, 5*(9), 524–528. Available at: https://doi.org/10.21276/ijre.2018.5.9.5.
7. Trovati, M., et al., (2015). *Big-Data Analytics and Cloud Computing*. PDFDRIVE. Springer. Available at: https://www.pdfdrive.com/big-data-analytics-and-cloud-computing-d28068060.html (accessed on 04 March 2023).

CHAPTER 6

TESTING WEB APPLICATIONS

UNIT INTRODUCTION

In the previous unit, we discussed the definition of big data, including with history of big data. Also, we discussed the analyst's perspective on data repositories, the characteristics of big data, and the types of big data analytics. We discussed the big data importance and applications of big data analytics; we discussed in the previous chapter.

In the present unit, we will extend our discussion on testing web applications. In this chapter, we will find the challenges and perspectives of web application testing and also discuss the approach to integration testing of a web application, test tool web, and problems in testing web applications. Furthermore, we will discuss this in this chapter.

One of the fastest-growing segments of software today is web apps. Web applications offer us new application types and a completely new method of distributing software to users. Web applications are used to develop highly interactive applications that have very high-quality requirements.

Web applications use a variety of new languages, technologies, and programming models. Modern web apps are complicated, interactive programs with intricate GUIs and various back-end software components combined uniquely and fascinatingly.

Software developers and academics face various new hurdles when analyzing, modeling, and testing these applications. Web applications are significantly more complex than straightforward HTML Web pages, including more than simply the front-end graphical user interfaces of those consumers. Instead, GUIs are constructed using HTML as the frontends of arbitrarily complex back-end software applications. According to Nielsen, interfaces (HTML) made up nearly all Web apps in 1995, almost 90% in 1998, and only approximately 50% of Web applications in 2000.

Compared to the user interfaces, the back-end software has been and continues to be growing in size and complexity. Since Web software applications are inherently heterogeneous, this presents a technological barrier.

Software components incorporate new components, used components, and third-party created Components off the Shelf. They are written in various languages, based on various programming models, and run on various hardware and software platforms (COTS).

Can components written in procedural, OO, interpreted, and hybrid languages like JSP be used to create a single Web application? Browsers, embedded scripting languages, and applets are examples of user-side technologies.

Examples of server-side technologies include HTML, CGI, Java server pages (JSPs), Java Servlets, and .NET technologies. They all communicate with different software parts, middleware, and database servers. These additional elements could be found on the client, the server, or other machines that are "behind" the server.

This variability makes it challenging to model and assess the integration's complexity. The heterogeneous nature of the software and the dispersed deployment bring on software difficulties that need to be managed during testing. Web applications can create various GUIs "on demand" depending on user inputs, user states, and server states, which is a more profound capability.

Standard GUI programs have totally static GUIs, and traditional GUI testing methods do not address some dynamic complications our methodologies attempt to address. The heterogeneous nature of Web applications also impacts how software components are connected.

Since at least the 1970s, the phrase "software coupling" has been used, and it is widely acknowledged that "less" coupling is preferable. Wu, Offutt, and Du defined Web software coupling as follows. The word "method" can be used to refer to functions, processes, subprograms, and methods in general.

A program has tight coupling if dependencies between methods are represented in the method's logic. In other words, if a calls B, a change in A might require the logical structure of B to be changed. When dependencies between methods are represented in a program's structure, and data flows, including definitions in callers and use in callees, this is called loose coupling.

Therefore, if A calls B, a change in A may cause the data structure to change, necessitating changes in how B uses data items defined in A. This type of connection is typically used in conjunction with data abstraction and information concealment.

When relationships between procedures are wholly stored in the data being transferred rather than in the structure, a program is said to have a very loose coupling (ELC). If A sends data to B, a change in A might change the contents of the data that B uses but not the structure of the data.

Due to the diverse nature of the software and the N-tier structure of most Web applications, ELC is essential to the success of the applications. Often, the only communication between developers is an awareness of the input and output requirements for the other component or an agreement on those requirements (for example, through an API).

Without having a complete understanding of how connected components interact, components are changed, added, and replaced. Even more so than before, software components can now be dynamically altered as new Web services are added, or existing ones are decommissioned.

Although this extremely loose and dynamic coupling gives developers strong abstraction capabilities, it makes the analysis necessary for testing quite challenging.

Learning Objectives

Following the completion of the chapter, the students should be able to understand the following:

- Understand the example of web applications and their testing – challenges and perspective;
- Understand the functional and Nonfunctional requirements of a web application;
- Understand the approach to integration testing of the web application;
- Understand the tool test web;
- Understand the problems in testing web applications.

Key Terms

- Application
- Integration
- Testing
- Approach
- Interaction
- Generating

6.1. WEB APPLICATION TESTING: CHALLENGES AND PERSPECTIVES

The objectives and functionality provided by web apps, as well as the technologies used to build them, have changed significantly since the Web's beginnings. Early Web apps were made up of a few simple static HTML pages.

However, more recent applications give their users a variety of tools for working with data, accessing databases, and doing several useful tasks. Most of the time, these tasks are carried out by software components built using proprietary technologies like Microsoft's active server pages (ASP) or JSP, Java Servlets, PHP, CGI, XML, ODBC, or JDBC (ASP).

KEYWORD

Java servlets are server-side programs (running inside a web server) that handle clients' requests and return a customized or dynamic response for each request.

These components take advantage of a complicated, heterogeneous execution environment comprising middleware, software, and hardware elements. The term "Web application" (or "application" in this chapter) refers to the collection of software components that implement the functionality and services that an application offers to its users, whereas the term "running environment" refers to the entire infrastructure (composed of hardware, software, and middleware components) required to run a Web application.

The main objective of testing a Web application is to use different input and state combinations to run the application and find errors. Failure occurs when a system or component is clearly unable to carry out a necessary task while meeting the required performance standards.

Faults in the application's implementation are responsible for failures. In general, there will be failures that are mostly brought on by flaws in the application itself and failures that are primarily brought on by flaws in the running environment or in the interface between the application and the environment on which it operates.

It is impossible to test a Web application independently to determine exactly which component is to blame for each exhibited failure because it is tightly integrated with the environment in which it runs. Various testing methods must be used to find these many forms of failures.

For example, performance, stability, and compatibility are examples of non-functional needs of a Web application that are most impacted by the operating environment, whereas the program handles functional requirements. Web application testing must therefore be seen from two different perspectives. According to one viewpoint, several testing techniques must be used to determine whether a Web application complies with predetermined non-functional requirements.

The opposing viewpoint looks at the challenge of testing an application's functional requirements. Since they complement one another and are not mutually exclusive, testing an application from both perspectives is essential.

6.1.1. Testing the Non-Functional Requirements of a Web Application

There are various non-functional requirements that a Web application must typically meet, either explicitly or implicitly. Designing testing activities with distinct objectives for each nonfunctional need is necessary. The verification procedures that can be used to test the primary non-functional requirements of a web application are described in subsections.

KEYWORD

Performance testing is a non-functional software testing technique that determines how the stability, speed, scalability, and responsiveness of an application holds up under a given workload.

6.1.1.1. Performance Testing

Performance testing confirms a system's expected performance (e.g., response time, service availability). Usually, performance testing is carried out by simulating many concurrent user accesses over a predetermined period. Information concerning accesses is first recorded and then analyzed to estimate the load levels that deplete the system's resources. System performance is crucial for Web applications because consumers expect services to be available at all times and do not want to wait for too long to receive responses to their requests. As it is impossible to predict in advance how many people will actually be logged into a live operating program, effective performance testing of Web applications is an essential undertaking. As a result, it is important to think of performance testing as a continuous process that should be carried out by analyzing data from access log files in order to properly tune the system.

Even though any software component of the application level, i.e., components implementing any business rule by non-optimized algorithms, may contribute to inefficiency, failures that can be found by performance testing are primarily caused by running environment faults (e.g., scarce resources, poorly deployed resources).

6.1.1.2. Load Testing

Although the terms "load testing" and "performance is testing" are sometimes used interchangeably, the former demands that system performance be measured at a predefined load level. It aims to determine how long it takes to complete various jobs and functions under certain circumstances.

These predetermined requirements include the operating application's minimum configuration and maximum activity levels. Additionally, in this instance, several concurrent user accesses are simulated. Information is recorded when the tasks are not completed within the allotted time frames, and failure reports are generated.

When performing load testing for Web applications, comparable considerations to those made for performance testing can also be considered. Issues with the operating environment cause most failures discovered during load testing.

KEYWORD

Stress testing is a computer-simulated technique to analyze how banks and investment portfolios fare in drastic economic scenarios.

6.1.1.3. Stress Testing

Stress testing is used to evaluate a system or component at or above the specifications' limits. It is employed to gauge how the system responds to activity surges that may exceed its capacity and to determine whether it crashes or is able to recover from such circumstances.

Stress testing differs from performance and load testing because it pushes the system to the limit, whereas performance and load testing simulate daily user activity. The challenges of stress testing for Web applications are comparable to those encountered during performance and load testing. Issues with the operating environment cause the majority of stress testing failures.

6.1.1.4. Compatibility Testing

Compatibility testing is done to see if an application functions as intended in an operating environment with different hardware, software, and middleware configurations. Regarding Web applications, compatibility testing must identify errors brought on using various Web server platforms or client browsers and match releases or configurations.

Testing every potential combination of components used to execute a Web application is not practical, so only the most prevalent combinations are typically considered. As such, only a portion of potential compatibility issues might be found. Failures in compatibility may result from either the program or the operating system. A general rule for preventing compatibility failures is to give users of Web applications the right information about the intended configuration of the running environment and the right diagnostic messages to deal with any identified incompatibilities.

6.1.1.5. Usability Testing

Usability testing is conducted to determine how user-friendly an application is. Usability is frequently impacted by both the user interface's design and execution. Usability testing is therefore primarily focused on evaluating the user interface, including concerns with the proper content rendering (such as graphics and text editing formats) as well as the clarity of messages, prompts, and commands that need to be taken into account and verified.

KEYWORD

Usability testing refers to evaluating a product or service by testing it with representative users.

Usability is a critical issue for a Web application. Indeed, it may determine the success of the application. As a result, throughout the creation of an application, the front end and how users interact with it are frequently factors that are given additional care and attention.

Usability testing of web applications considers and verifies difficulties with an application's navigation accuracy, thoroughness, and conciseness. This kind of testing should constantly enhance a Web application's usability; user profiling techniques are typically employed to accomplish this goal. The application is primarily to blame for usability issues.

6.1.1.6. Accessibility Testing

Accessibility testing is a specific kind of usability testing whose aim is to confirm that access to an application's content is allowed even in the presence of limited hardware and software configurations on the client side (for example, browser configurations disabling graphical visualization or scripting execution) or in the presence of users with disabilities, such as visual impairment.

In the case of Web applications, accessibility rules such as the one provided by the Web Content Accessibility Guidelines have been established so that accessibility testing represents verification of the compliance of an application with such rules. The application itself is generally the main cause of accessibility problems, even when accessibility failures may be due to the configuration of the running environment (e.g., browsers where the execution of scripts is disabled).

6.1.1.7. Security Testing

Security testing aims to verify the effectiveness of the overall Web application's defenses against undesired access of unauthorized users, its capability to preserve system resources from improper use, and granting authorized users access to authorized services and resources.

Application defenses have to provide protection mechanisms able to avoid or reduce damage due to intrusions, with costs that should be significantly less than damages caused by a security break. Application vulnerabilities affecting security may be contained in the application code or any different hardware, software, and middleware components.

Remember

On the other hand, the authors used automaton and composition of automata that are interactions between components.

Both the running environment and the application can be responsible for security failures. In the case of Web applications, heterogeneous implementations, and execution technologies, together with the very large number of possible users and the possibility of accessing them from anywhere, can make Web applications more vulnerable than traditional applications and security testing more difficult to accomplish.

6.1.2. Testing the Functional Requirements of a Web Application

Testing the functional requirements of an application aims to verify that its features and operational behavior correspond to its specifications. In other words, this type of testing is responsible for uncovering application failures due to faults in the functional requirements' implementation rather than failures due to the application's running environment.

To achieve this aim, any failures due to the running environment should be avoided or reduced to a minimum. Preliminary assumptions about the running environment will have to be made before test design and execution. Most methods and approaches used to test the functional requirements of "traditional" software can also be used for Web applications. Similarly to traditional software testing, a Web application's functionality testing has to rely on the following basic aspects:

- Testing levels specify the different scope of the tests to be carried out, i.e., the collections of components to be tested.
- Test strategies, which define heuristics or algorithms to create test cases from software representation models, implementation models, or test models.
- Test models represent the relationships between a representation's elements or a component's implementation.
- Testing processes define the flow of testing activities and other decisions such as when to start testing, which is to perform the testing, how much effort should be used, etc.

However, despite their similarity to conventional applications, Web applications also have distinguishing features that cause specific problems for each aspect described in the previous list. For example, the definition of testing levels for a Web application requires greater attention than that applied to traditional software.

KEYWORD

Data flow is a fully managed streaming analytics service that minimizes latency, processing time, and cost through autoscaling and batch processing.

At the unit testing level, the scope of a unit test cannot be defined uniquely since it depends on the existence of different types of components (e.g., Web pages, script functions, embedded objects) residing on both the client and server side of an application.

In relation to integration testing, the numerous different mechanisms used to integrate an application's heterogeneous and distributed components can generate several coupling levels, and data flow between the components, which have to be considered to establish a correct integration strategy.

As for the strategies for test design, the classical approaches of black box, white box, or gray box testing may be considered for designing test cases, provided that preliminary considerations are defined. In general, Web applications' black box testing will not differ from software applications' black box testing.

In both cases, using a predetermined coverage criterion, an adequate set of test cases is defined based on the specified functionality of the item to be tested. However, a Web application's specific features can affect test design and execution.

For example, testing components dynamically generated by the running application can be very expensive due to the difficulty of identifying and regenerating the same conditions that produced each component. Therefore, traditional testing models used to represent the behavior of an application may have to be adapted to these characteristics and the Web applications' running environment.

White box testing, irrespective of an application's nature, is usually based on coverage criteria considering the application's structural features or components.

Adequate models representing an application or component's structure are used, and coverage criteria and test cases are appropriately specified. White box testing aims to cover the structural elements considered.

Since the architecture and components of a Web application are largely different from those of a traditional application, appropriate models representing structural information at different levels of granularity and abstraction are needed, and coverage criteria have to be defined accordingly.

KEYWORD

Gray-box testing is a combination of white-box testing and black-box testing.

For example, models representing navigation, as well as traditional structural aspects of an application, need to be taken into account. Coverage criteria must focus both on hyperlinks, which allow user navigation in the application and on inner items of an application's component (e.g., its code statements).

Besides black and white box testing, gray box testing can also be considered for Web applications. Grey box testing is a mixture of black and white box testing. It considers both the application's behavior from the end user's viewpoint (same as black box testing) and the application's inner structure and technology (same as white box testing).

Gray box testing is suitable for testing Web applications because it factors in high-level design, environment, and interoperability conditions. This type of testing is expected to reveal problems that are not easily identified by the black box or white box analysis, particularly problems related to end-to-end information flow and distributed hardware/software system configuration and compatibility.

Context-specific failures are relevant to Web applications are commonly uncovered using gray-box testing. Finally, for the testing processes, the classical approach for testing execution that starts from unit testing and proceeds with integration, system testing, and acceptance testing can also be considered for Web applications.

For each phase, however, differences with respect to testing traditional software have to be detected, and specific solutions have to be designed. An important testing process issue is, for instance, setting up an environment to execute tests at each phase: driver or stub modules are usually required to run tests at the unit or integration phase. Solutions for testing a Web application must explicitly consider the application's distributed running environment and adopt the necessary communication mechanisms for executing the tested components.

6.2. AN APPROACH TO INTEGRATION TESTING OF WEB APPLICATIONS

Differently from traditional software, where white-box testing is typically applied only at the unit level, for Web applications, it is possible to exploit the knowledge on the organization of the system into server programs, dynamic pages, forms, links, etc., to define integration testing criteria (Figure 6.1).

Figure 6.1. *Bug finding testing.*

Source: Image by Max Pixel.

The proposed approach's starting point is the Web application's UML model. The determination of this model is not a trivial task. First of all, it should be noted that recovering the implicit-state model is a much harder task than recovering the explicit-state one.

In fact, in the implicit-state model, the behavior of each server program and the content of dynamic pages depend on conditions associated with the outgoing edges that have to be specified by the user (it is not possible recovering them) and must be complete and consistent.

For large sites, the task of their specification is not affordable in practice. Moreover, when the UML model is exploited for coverage assessment and test case generation, it is not easy (in general, it is undecidable) to determine whether a selected path is feasible (i.e., there exists an input such that all edge conditions in the path evaluate to true).

On the contrary, recovering the explicit-state model is more practical, and all the paths in this model are feasible by construction. The operation performed on a Web application to extract its explicit-state model is called state unrolling.

It consists of replicating each server program and dynamic page that is accessed in a new state, i.e., with inputs belonging to an equivalence class or with hidden state variables or parameters associated with a state never encountered before.

This operation cannot be fully automated. The user's intervention consists of specifying a sample input for every application behavior. Then, the remaining steps of model extraction can be automated.

KEYWORD

Server program is a program that enables a user to perform tasks on a computer in order to connect to other programs or resources.

In fact, when a server program is executed, and a dynamic page is retrieved, it is possible to automatically check if the related state is new or it was encountered previously, thus deciding whether to unroll it or not.

The model obtained through the state unrolling operation is a conservative explicit state model, which may include more expansions than is strictly required. In fact, it may happen that a given server program P_1 behaves differently in the two states, S_1 and S_2, while the server program P_2 has exactly the same behavior in the two states.

According to the unrolling procedure described above, P_2 is split into two because it is accessed in two distinct states. A second operation, called state merging, is applied to unify the server programs and dynamic pages that in different states behave the same.

In general, assessing the behavioral equivalence of two software modules is undecidable, but in our case, some heuristics can be applied to the simplest cases. For example, when the resulting dynamic pages are exactly the same, it is possible to unify them, as well as the unrolled server programs that generated them, since they give the same result in the two different states.

More complex cases of state merging are associated with generating dynamic pages with a common structure but different contents and with generating dynamic pages in which the structure has some regularity that suggests a common behavior.

User intervention in these cases is unavoidable. The recovered model of the Web application represents its internal structure, which can be accessed to measure the coverage that a given test suite (collection of test cases) reaches with respect to a given test criterion (stating the features to be tested).

A test case for a Web application is a sequence of pages to be visited plus the input values to be provided to pages containing forms. Therefore, it can be represented as a sequence of URLs specifying the pages to ask and, if needed, the values to assign to the input variables.

Execution consists of requesting the Web server for the URLs in the sequence and storing the output pages. Differently from traditional software, branch selection can be forced by choosing the associated hyperlink without tracking conditions back to input values. Some white box testing criteria, derived from those available for traditional software (Beizer, 1990), are:

- **Page Testing:** Every page in the web application is visited at least once in some test cases.
- **Hyperlink Testing:** Every hyperlink from every page is traversed at least once.
- **Definition-Use Testing:** All navigation paths from every definition of a variable to every use of it, forming data dependence, are exercised.
- **All-Uses Testing:** At least one navigation path from every definition of a variable to every use of it, forming data dependence, is exercised.
- **All-Paths Testing:** Every path in the Web application is traversed in some test case at least once.

Flow analyses can be employed to determine the data dependencies required by some testing criteria. Nodes of kind Form generate a definition of each variable in the input set. Such definitions are propagated along the edges of the Web site graph.

If a definition of a variable reaches a node where the same variable is used (use an attribute of a dynamic page) along a definition-clear path, there is data dependence between defining node and the user node. The definition-use and all-paths criteria are often impractical since a site typically has infinite paths if loops are present.

They can be satisfied if weaker constraints are imposed on the paths to be considered. Examples are loop k-limiting and path independence. Loops are traversed at least k times in the first case, while only independent paths are considered in the second

KEYWORD

White box testing is a form of application testing that provides the tester with complete knowledge of the application being tested, including access to source code and design documents.

case. A path is independent of a given set of paths if its vector representation is linearly independent of any other path in the set.

Not all pages are equally interesting when designing and executing test cases for a Web application. Static pages not containing forms can be disregarded since they do not collect user input, process it or display results.

TIPS

The structure of the software design is usually different from traditional software, the software components are integrated in different ways, and the components communicate in unusual ways and Web applications use new software technologies such as session management.

They contain fixed information that needs not be examined during dynamic validation. The site can thus be reduced while retaining only the relevant entities. Given the graph representation of a Web application, a reduced graph can be computed for white box testing. Each static page without forms is removed from the graph, and all its predecessors (if any) are linked to all its successors.

In the resulting graph, a fictitious entry node is added, connected with all nodes with no predecessor. A fictitious exit node is directly reachable from all output nodes, i.e., dynamic nodes with non-empty use attributes.

In a Web application, the end of computation is reached when some result is displayed to the user, but no intrinsic notion of termination for a navigation session exists. Therefore, dynamic pages whose content depends on the user input are good candidates for ending meaningful computations.

6.2.1. Test Case Generation

Satisfaction with any of the white box testing criteria involves selecting a set of paths in the Web application graph and providing input values. In the explicit-state model, path selection is independent of input values and can be automated.

Moreover, since in the explicit-state model, edges are associated with the actual inputs used to recover the model, given a path of interest, it is easy to determine the inputs that allow traversing it. They can be just collected from the path edges.

Note that the same operation in the implicit-state model is much harder because it involves determining inputs that satisfy the path condition, i.e., the conjunction of the conditions in the path edges. We propose a test case generation technique based on the computation of the reduced Web site graph's path expression (Beizer, 1990). A path expression is an algebraic representation of the paths in a graph. Variables in a path expression are edge labels. They can be combined through operators + and $*$, associated, respectively, with selection and loop. Brackets can be used to group sub-expressions.

link (build (submit$_1$ + submit$_2$ + submit$_3$)) $*$ link build$_1$ submit$_1$ build$_2$ (submit$_2$ build$_3$ + submit$_3$ build$_4$)

When edges have been indexed with a numeric identifier when necessary to distinguish them, the Computation of the path expression for a site can be performed using the Node-Reduction algorithm described by Beizer (1990).

Since the path expression directly represents all paths in the graph, it can be employed to generate sequences of nodes (test cases) that satisfy any of the coverage criteria. Determining the minimum number of paths from a path expression and satisfying a given criterion is generally a hard task. However, heuristics can be defined to compute an approximation of the minimum.

KEYWORD

Heuristics are mental shortcuts that allow people to solve problems and make judgments quickly and efficiently.

The heuristic technique adopted for this work is based on the following scheme. While the criterion is not satisfied for each alternative from inner to outer nesting, choose one never considered before, if any, or randomly choose one of the computed paths that increase coverage and add it to the resulting paths where the alternative for a loop is whether to reiterate or not.

Definition-use and all-uses testing can be achieved by considering the definition as the entry node for each data dependence and the use as the exit of the sub-graph to be tested. Criteria such as definition-use and all-paths testing, requiring the coverage of all paths, can be met only if restricted to independent or k-limited paths.

Once paths for the test cases are generated from the path expression, the related input values can be obtained from the attributes of the edges in the explicit-state model used for test case generation. Then, their execution can be automated, and after downloading, the output pages can be inspected to assess whether the test case was passed or not.

Regression testing highly benefits from the automation described above since each test case can be executed unattended on a new Web application version. Its output pages can be automatically compared with those obtained from a run of the previous version.

6.2.2. Modeling Database Interactions in Web Applications and Generating Test Cases

In this part, it is explained that the authors propose Generating test cases from modeling database interaction in web applications. They used a minimal test set to generate tests. Also, they propose an algorithm that decreases the overlap to optimize test paths.

Guarded finite state machines (GFSM) that are improved FSMs and guarded finite state machines test tree (GFSMTT) is used. The authors achieved a minimal test set from the test tree for generating the test. Also, they proposed an algorithm that can optimize the test paths with declining overlap. So they can decrease the timely manner. Also, they used FSM and mixed it with mathematical relations in the "modeling tool" part. The authors generate test cases from modeling database interactions. They used GFSM and GFSMTT for their proposed approach. So, they work on database relations and interactions in the program's structure.

Remember

Testing is responsible for uncovering application failures due to faults in the functional requirements' implementation, rather than failures due to the application's running environment.

The authors prepared test cases and modeled database interactions in web applications. They used GFSM and GFSMTT, and they have a functional assessment in their proposed approach. Also, they proposed an algorithm that creates a minimum test set of GFSMTT. Lastly, they proposed an algorithm that declines the overlap for optimizing the test path and improving the quality of their work.

6.2.3. Testing a Web Application Involving Web Browser Interaction

In several research studies/papers, the authors proposed testing web applications based on web browser interaction. They proposed an approach to find out the inconsistencies between the web pages' properties and the web browsers' buttons.

Finite state machines (FSM) are used in this approach. They used mathematical definitions and relations for preparing a navigation tree in the "construct a navigation tree" part. They enter input and see each input's output and result, and they are not concerned about any program structure or internal actions and behavior.

They tested web applications with the interactions of a web browser. During preparing the navigation tree, all the inputs, outputs, and results of the web browser are considered (Figure 6.2).

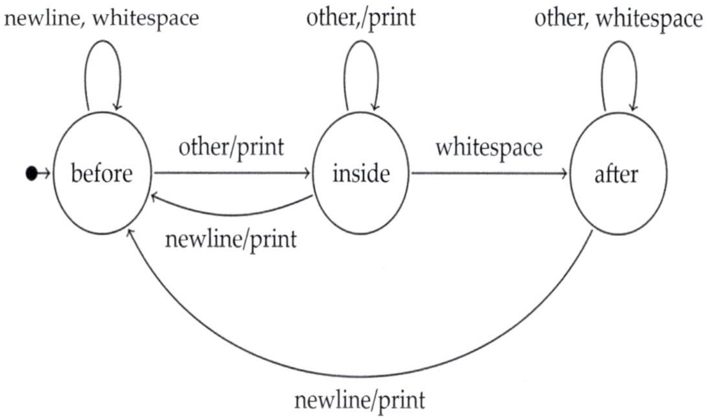

Figure 6.2. *Finite state machine.*

Source: Image by Wikimedia Commons.

6.2.4. User Acceptance Testing (UAT) of Web Applications

Many authors proposed a call for testing (CFT), which is a new test model. To perform user acceptance testing (UAT), they develop adequate testing techniques for all the testers. Also, they build a testing auditing mechanism.

They proposed that remove a non-leaf node from the graph and combining the edge starting and edge ending of the removed node. Finally, the leaf and root nodes will remain. So, with this idea, the timely manner will be declined.

They suggested that customers and end-users should test their approach through beta testing. It means that customers want to take correct results and output anywhere. Also, for generating paths, they consider internal actions and structures of the program.

They focus on input and output data. Also, for generating path, the authors focus on processes and want to decrease processes for getting better timely manner.

6.2.5. An Approach to Generating Test Cases for Testing Component-Based Web Applications

In this chapter, the authors propose Generating test cases from component-based web applications. With the assumption of a logic component (LC) and a web application that includes LCs, and each LC is a black box, they proposed an automaton for modeling each component and compositions of automata for modeling the interactions between components. Logical component (LC), black box testing, automaton, and compositions of automata are used, and various authors assumed that each logical component and component is black box tested. Then they focus on testing the interactions between components.

So, web applications are set of components and logical components, and with the assumption of black box testing for each component and logical component, the timely manner will be decreased automatically. They used mathematical definitions to specify the actions of a component in the "the actions of the component" part.

KEYWORD

Black-box testing is a method of software testing that examines the functionality of an application without peering into its internal structures or workings.

In black box testing, only input and output data are concerned. On the other hand, the authors used automaton and composition of automata, which are interactions between components. If the output of a component is communicated to the input of another component, it means there is an interaction between these two components.

Also, they used automaton and composition of automata that are interactions between components and is considered as functional testing.

6.2.6. An Approach to Modeling and Testing Web Applications Based on Use Cases

With UCTM, they implement a method for testing system levels by moving the explanation of each use case into CDD (constraint directed diagram). Then they suggested CSC (constraint scenario coverage). They generated test cases from CDD that can assure the criterion of CSC.

Hierarchical profile use case diagrams with the name of use case transition models (UCTM) and logical components are used in this approach. The authors used mathematical definitions for creating test cases in the "generating test cases" part.

Also, they used UML and use case diagrams in their approach. They used UML, use case diagrams, UCTM, LC, CDD, and CSC, and all of them tested functional targets of testing. Also, in their model, they can execute simultaneously if the two use cases do not depend on each other. So, the testing time can be deducted, and the testing efficiency can be enhanced.

ACTIVITY 6.1.

WebApp Planning-In-House Web Engineering

The steps that follow are recommended for small and moderately- sized WebE projects:

- Understand scope, the dimensions of change, and project constraints.
- Define an incremental project strategy. The team establishes a project strategy that defines web app increments (releases) that provide useful content and functionality for end-users. Engineering effort can then be more effectively focused.
- Perform risk analysis.

6.3. THE TOOL TEST WEB

The UML model of the Web application to be analyzed is generated by the other tool we are developing, ReWeb. Among the others, ReWeb contains a module called Spider, which downloads all pages of a target web site starting from a given URL.

Each page found within the site host is downloaded and marked with the date of downloading. The HTML documents outside the web site host are not considered. The pages of a site are obtained by sending the associated requests to the Web server. For dynamic pages, the user has to specify the set of inputs that the Spider will provide to the server programs generating them.

To obtain an explicit-state model representing all server program behaviors, the user can provide more inputs associated with the same dynamic page. The resulting UML model is an explicit-state model in which server programs and dynamic pages have been unrolled according to all different conditions specified by the user in terms of different input values.

The operation of state merging is currently performed manually, but some strategies for its partial automation can be implemented. They have been sketched in the previous section. The Spider will not expand the model beyond the related server program if no input is specified for a given dynamic page.

This feature of ReWeb is useful for analyzing the functioning of portions of a Web application. Partitioning the tested functionalities by cutting the model at given nodes is important, especially for large Web applications. The user also has to provide the set of used variables, use, for each dynamic page whose content depends on some input value. Such a property is necessary for data-flow testing. Test Web contains a test case generation engine (Test generator), able to determine the path expression from a Web application's model and generate test cases from it provided that a test criterion is specified. Generated test cases are sequences of URLs that, once executed, grant the coverage of the selected criterion. Input values in each URL sequence are those specified for the Spider. Such inputs can be marked with the unrolling index of the server program and dynamic page they allow to download. In this way, it is possible to obtain exactly the dynamic page with the structure required to follow a given path during testing.

In fact, a page with the needed structure was obtained by the Spider by providing the same input values. Such a possibility solves one of the major problems in testing traditional software: selecting the inputs to traverse a path of interest. Testing Web applications is simpler because branch selection can be forced, being associated with the user navigation, which is an external input. Moreover, the existence of the hyperlink to be followed is granted if the dynamic page is obtained under the same conditions in which it was downloaded.

TIPS

Stress testing is used to evaluate the system's response at activity peaks that can exceed system limitations, and to verify if the system crashes or is able to recover from such conditions.

This can be achieved by exploiting the same inputs that the Spider uses. Test Web's Test executor can now provide the URL request sequence of each test case to the Web server, attaching proper inputs to each form.

The output pages produced by the server, marked in the UML model with a non-empty use attribute, are stored for further examination. After execution, the test engineer intervenes to assess each test case's pass/fail result. For such an evaluation, they open the output pages on a browser and check whether the output is correct for each given input. During regression check, such user intervention is no longer required since the oracle (expected output values) is the one produced (and manually checked) in a previous testing iteration. Of course, manual intervention is still required in the presence of discrepancies. A second numeric output of test case execution is the level of coverage reached by the current test suite.

6.4. PROBLEMS IN TESTING WEB APPLICATIONS

This part of the chapter defines a Web page to be information that can be viewed in a single browser window. A Web page may be stored as a static HTML file, or it may be dynamically generated by software such as JSP or Java Servlets.

A web site is a collection of Web pages and associated software components that are related semantically by content and syntactically through links and other control mechanisms. Web sites can be dynamic and interactive.

A web application is a program that runs in whole or in part on one or more Web servers, and users can run that through a Web site. The literature on testing Web applications is still scarce, and there is no widespread agreement on how to categorize the technical problems.

An important factor influencing Web applications is how the different pieces are connected. We make our initial attempts to categorize testing in terms of the following connections:

- **Static Links (HTML → HTML):** Most of the early literature on Web testing focused on link validation. Note that this does not address any software or dynamic issues.
- **Dynamic Links (HTML → Software):** HTML forms send data to software components that process the data. One issue with testing dynamic links is that data must be found or created for the forms.
- **Dynamically Created HTML (Software → HTML):** Web software typically responds to the user with HTML documents. The contents of the HTML documents often depend on inputs, which complicates testing.
- **User/Time Specific GUIs (Software + State → HTML):** HTML documents whose contents and form are determined by not just inputs but some state of the server, such as the data or time, the user, or session information.
- **Operational Transitions (User):** Transitions that the user introduces into the system outside of the control of the HTML or software. Operational transitions include using the back button, the forward button, and URL rewriting.
- **Software Connections:** This includes connections among back-end software components, such as method calls and forwarding among Web components.
- **Off-Site Software Connections:** Some web applications will access software components that are available at a remote site. This type of connection, while powerful, is

KEYWORD

HTML is the standard markup language for documents designed to be displayed in a web browser.

difficult to test because little is known about the off-site software.

- **Dynamic Connections:** Both the J2EE platform and .NET allow new Web components to be installed dynamically during execution, and the Web application can detect and use the new components. J2EE uses Java reflection and Java beans to accomplish this. This type of connection is especially difficult to test because the tester does not know how the components will behave before deployment and execution.

This chapter addresses the problem of black box systems or application testing of Web applications. Our approach applies test criteria to a structured model of the application. Tests for entire Web applications are created by composing sub-tests derived from models of lower-level abstractions of the applications.

Did you Know?

In other words, this type of testing is responsible for uncovering application failures due to faults in the functional requirements' implementation, rather than failures due to the application's running environment.

The primary focus is on the state dependent behavior of Web applications. FSM provides a convenient way to model software behavior in a way that avoids issues associated with the implementation.

Several methods for deriving tests from FSMs have also been proposed. Theoretically, Web applications can be completely modeled with FSMs; however, even simple Web pages can suffer from the state space explosion problem.

There can be a large variety of possible inputs to text fields, a large number of options on some Web pages, and choices as to the order in which information can be entered. Factors such as these mean that a finite state machine can become prohibitively large, even for a single page.

Thus, an FSM-based testing method can only be used if techniques are found to generate FSMs that are descriptive enough to yield effective tests yet small enough to be practically useful. The technique, FSMWeb, addresses the state explosion problem with a hierarchical collection of aggregated FSMs.

The bottom-level FSMs are formed from Web pages and parts of Web pages called logical Web pages, and the top-level FSM represents the entire Web application. Application level tests are formed by combining test sequences from lower-level FSMs.

To allow the combined test sequences to be meaningful, constraints on parameter values that are propagated from earlier parts of the sequence are expressed.

SUMMARY

- **Web Application Testing:** This chapter summarizes about the challenges and perspectives in web application testing. The functional and non-functional requirements of web applications have also been discussed in this chapter.
- **Approach to Integration Testing of Web Applications:** This part of the chapter focuses on the approach to integration testing of web applications. Different approaches are – test case generation, Modeling database interactions in web applicants, testing a web application involving web browser interaction, UAT of web applications, an approach to generating test cases for testing component-based web applications, and an approach to modeling and testing web applications based on use cases. The tool test web, Problems in testing Web applications have also been discussed in this chapter.

REVIEW QUESTIONS

1. What are the challenges and perspectives in web application testing?
2. Explain the course student information system (CSIS)?
3. What is test case generation?
4. Explain the functional and non-functional requirements of a web application?
5. What is a tool test web?
6. What are the problems in testing web applications?

MULTIPLE CHOICE QUESTIONS

1. Which of the following is not a Web app interface mechanism?

a. Browser
b. Cookies
c. Forms
d. Links

2. Which of the following is not a testable Web app security element?

a. Authentication
b. Encryption
c. Firewalls
d. Penetration

3. Web app performance tests are designed to:

a. Assess web app usability

b. Evaluate page loading times
c. Simulate real-world loading situations
d. Test network connectivity

4. Standard Enforcer is a:

a. Static testing tool
b. Dynamic testing
c. Static and dynamic testing
d. None of the above

5. CSIS Stands for:

a. Course student information system
b. Courses simulate information system
c. Course structure information system
d. None

Answers to Multiple Choice Questions

1. (c) 2. (d) 3. (c) 4. (a) 5. (a)

REFERENCES

1. Andrews, A. A., Offutt, J., & Alexander, R. T., (n.d). *Testing Web Applications by Modeling with FSMs*. cs.gmu.edu.gmu. Available at: https://cs.gmu.edu/~offutt/rsrch/papers/webtest.pdf (accessed on 04 March 2023).
2. Athaiya, S., & Komondoor, R., (2017). *Testing and Analysis of Web Applications Using Page Models – CSA*. www.csa.iisc.ac.in. International Symposium on Software Testing and Analysis. Available at: https://www.csa.iisc.ac.in/~raghavan/ReadingMaterial/issta2017-paper.pdf (accessed on 04 March 2023).
3. Di Lucca, G. A., & Fasolino, A. R., (2006). Web application testing. *Web Engineering*, 219–260. Available at: https://doi.org/10.1007/3-540-28218-1_7.
4. Dogan, S., Betin-Can, A., & Garousi, V., (2014). *Web Application Testing: A Systematic Literature Review*. romisatriawahono.net. Elsevier Inc. Available at: https://romisatriawahono.net/lecture/rm/survey/software%20engineering/Software%20Testing/Dogan%20-%20Web%20App%20Testing%20-%202014.pdf (accessed on 04 March 2023).
5. Jaleel, H. Q., (2019). Testing web applications. *International Journal of Computer Science and Engineering, 6*(12), 1–9. Available at: https://doi.org/10.14445/23488387/ijcse-v6i12p101.

6. Nikfard, P., (2014). *Testing on Web Applications, National Software Engineering Conference*. academia. Available at: https://www.academia.edu/3790158/Testing_on_web_applications (accessed on 04 March 2023).
7. Ricca, F., & Tonella, P., (2002). *Testing Processes of Web Applications*. www.ecs.csun.edu. Kluwer Academic Publishers. Available at: https://www.ecs.csun.edu/~rlingard/COMP595VAV/RiccaPaper.pdf (accessed on 04 March 2023).
8. Slack, J. M., (2011). System testing of desktop and web applications. files.eric.ed.gov. *Information Systems Education Journal*. Available at: https://files.eric.ed.gov/fulltext/EJ1145469.pdf (accessed on 04 March 2023).

CHAPTER 7

WEB PROJECT MANAGEMENT

UNIT INTRODUCTION

Project information used in web-based applications must be managed and stored by web-based project management systems. Project apps will provide separate groups of workers, such as the seals department, programmers, or project managers, to have regulated access to information and automated delivery of information.

The goal of collaboration has been to accomplish tasks more quickly, inexpensively, and effectively by applying their shared expertise and combining various resources and accomplishments in a project. Since effective teamwork increases output, accelerates decision-making, and maximizes the ability to make the right choices, it also aids in saving valuable intellectual resources and time.

Surprisingly, a web-based project management system can increase company performance, productivity, and efficiency. There is no need for desktop installation or upgrades, as web-based programs are accessible through any online browser. Further, while staying in geographically distinct locations and maintaining team collaboration, engineers who generate excellent code while remaining invisible can use it across a distance.

The system's background provides an overview of the relevant field, as well as the driving forces behind the research and development. Project management is the process of organizing, scheduling, and directing project activities to achieve project goals.

Project management basically involves overseeing a project from the beginning to the end while achieving its objectives and aims. Currently, projects are more complex than ever before. Today's projects require "greater financial investments, more disciplines, geographically dispersed project partners, tighter schedules, more stringent quality requirements, etc."

In order to improve the efficacy of current project management techniques, these factors, along with quick advances in information and communication technology and the widespread use of outsourcing, have influenced project management practices to adopt new techniques and patterns brought about by new technology using new software and tools. In addition, effective communication between businesses and between clients and businesses is essential to achieving a project's goals.

New forms of communication have been made possible by new technology and revolutionary information technology (IT) innovations. This chapter will outline the development of project management as well as the difficulties and issues that contemporary project management techniques are now facing.

The impact of the most recent technological developments on project management will then be highlighted, with a special emphasis placed on the innovative fact of project management through the Internet. Finally, the advantages and benefits of web-enabling project management will be discussed while also highlighting significant drawbacks and limitations.

Learning Objectives

Following the completion of the chapter, the students should be able to understand the following:

- Understand the definitions, challenges, and limitations of project management;
- Understand the types of web based software for the construction industry;
- Understand the specifics of web projects;
- Understand the agile vs. traditional web project management;
- Understand web-based project management system;
- Understand the advantages and limitations of WPMS;
- Understand the utilization of WPMS in the construction industry;
- Learn how to manage the development process of a web application.

Key Terms

- Limitations
- Construction

- Enterprise
- Traditional
- Utilization
- Measuring
- Management

7.1. PROJECT MANAGEMENT (FIGURE 7.1)

Figure 7.1. *Project management.*

Source: Image by Pix4Free.

7.1.1. Definitions

PMI (2004) defines a project as "a transitory activity intended to generate a distinctive product or service." Projects exist until they achieve their goals and objectives and have definite beginning and ending dates (Heldman et al., 2007).

A project usually splits into smaller projects (sub-projects), produces a special good or service, is goal-oriented, and entails the coordinated completion of linked tasks (Brandon, 2005; Frame, 2005). According to PMI (2004), managing a project, formerly known as project management, is "the application of knowledge, skills, tools, and techniques to the project activities in order to meet or exceed stakeholder needs and expectations from a project."

It is accountable for the planning, organizing, monitoring, and control of all project components. It is also accountable for the management, inspiration, and motivation of all participants in order for the project to succeed (Brandon, 2005). Cost, performance, and time goals are the basic project management goals that must be achieved, and at the same time, the project's purpose must be controlled or maintained at a predetermined level (Lewis, 2001).

7.1.2. Challenges

Even though the term "project management" has been around for some time, difficulties still persist. The main obstacles to project management are discussed below:

- **Quality:** The handling of quality issues in projects can be challenging. Usually, a contractor or other third party is designated to oversee quality control. According to Amalraj et al. (2007), the parent company should be in charge of quality control and assurance. Additionally, it is said that the parent firm must examine and approve individual contractor quality plans at an early stage of the project plan. In order to avoid discrepancies between the initial plans and the final product, the project's development process and the quality contractor must occur concurrently.
- **Cost:** In many cases, initiatives begin with lower expected costs because there is a lack of cost knowledge. This occurs since a project that is more affordable is more appealing and more likely to get accepted in order to begin. Further, the clients also want high-quality goods and services at competitive prices. This impacts the project's cost plan, driving, in most circumstances, the project's true cost. The crucial point is that this typically influences the quality of the finished product or service (Alshawi & Ingirige, 2003).

TIPS

Modern-day web applications are prone to agile models, which produce the prototype, i.e., the first 'draft' of the application very quickly.

- **Environment and Complexity:** Project managers must consider the location, the time, the weather, and the moral climate in which the project will be developed and released. Depending on the location, there are various cultures, obstacles, and difficulties. As a project becomes more complex, communication between all parties involved becomes more difficult. As a result, the project needs to adhere to the norms and laws that govern it, and experts who can contribute to decision-making must be included (Amalraj et al., 2007; Alshawi & Ingirige, 2003).
- **Schedule:** Many businesses lack the necessary planners and schedulers for projects, which can cause issues with project schedules and productivity goals. A project's costs are less likely to exceed the budget if there is a well-defined schedule (Amalraj et al., 2007).
- **Unreal Targets:** Unrealistic or too ambitious project goals without the necessary resources and skills can delay project completion and put pressure on the project team, which lowers productivity (Amalraj et al., 2007).
- **Globalization of the Marketplace:** The removal of tariff barriers puts pressure on various industries, and the fact that each state's economy is at a different level makes this reality confusing. This can be difficult because some

overseas businesses can compete with domestic ones on price, quality, and delivery (Alshawi & Ingirige, 2003).

7.1.3. Limitations

Current project management techniques have several limits when it comes to effectively meeting the demands that have already been raised. These limitations are being addressed below:

KEYWORD

Purchasing is the organized acquisition of goods and services on behalf of the buying entity.

- **Lack of Adequate Communication:** Lack of effective communication among participants is the most prevalent issue project manager's encounter. According to Alshawi & Ingirige (2003), the current project management methods are frequently "isolated and concentrated with controlling challenges connected to different stages of the projects." Communication issues result in extra work or rework, which raises the project's cost. These are brought on by the conflicts brought about by information that is supplied inconsistently and at a different time than planned. The primary cause of this is the inconsistent information flow between the stakeholders involved in the project.
- **Lack of Integration Within the Supply Chain:** The procedures that businesses use to carry out their ordering, purchasing, and invoicing operations are hampered by the low-level supplier and manufacturer collaboration, low-level purchasing software integration, and delays in the delivery of supplies (Alshawi & Ingirige, 2003).
- **The Introduction of Automation into Management Practices:** Many businesses employ IT to enhance the management and quality of their goods, services, and operations. Although almost all businesses employ both traditional and electronic processes, there are frequent conflicts between the two that make it challenging for project managers to handle the appropriate information as and when required. This occurs not just due to a lack of training in the operation of automatic systems but also due to the differences in how information is given to humans and machines.
- **Lack of Software Integration:** Most IT systems solutions focus on particular tasks like project planning and monitoring, estimating, design, etc. Although there are no communication linkages between these apps, there is typically incompatibility between hardware and software

and a lack of integration of existing systems that allow for smooth information flow between the levels of project creation and maintenance (Alshawi, 2000; Faraj & Alshawi, 2000).

- **Lack of a Standardized Platform for Information Exchange:** Project managers may encounter some issues as a result of hardware and software incompatibilities while trying to access and handle project information. According to Alshawi & Ingirige (2003), the reason for these issues are "the lack of standardization of project information that can improve the flow of information between incompatible hardware and software."
- **Lack of Proper Decision-Making Tools for Project Planning:** Planning is a significant, challenging, and time-consuming process. If the project managers incorporate decision-making tools into their framework, Alshawi & Ingirige (2003) suggested that this process might be enhanced.
- **Lack of Standard Processes for Project Management:** Every project manager has their own set of rules, procedures, and methods that they employ, along with their own project management expertise. Therefore, a project's management can vary, and these practices can significantly impact a project's ability to coordinate and regulate its information (Alshawi & Ingirige, 2003).

KEYWORD

Project management is the application of processes, methods, skills, knowledge and experience to achieve specific project objectives according to the project acceptance criteria within agreed parameters.

7.2. THE SPECIFICS OF WEB PROJECTS

Building a corporate website is a multidisciplinary activity, requiring multiple skills necessary for completing highly heterogeneous tasks, such as data modeling, site interface modeling, hypertext modeling, designing a noticeable site appearance, compiling extensive high-performance architectures, or integrating inherent applications.

Building and maintaining these requires the implementation of software engineering tools and techniques, appropriate design concepts and methods, and a well-founded methodological framework enabling the appropriate management of all those development activities.

Building a corporate web site includes four components: content, form, function, and purpose. Opinions on how these components should be mutually ranged differ, so that the relative importance of each individual aspect differs from one project to another.

The common denominator of all projects is that they have their beginning and end (the time factor), with predefined quality and volume of costs, i.e., budget. To complete a project within such limitations, it is necessary to manage it appropriately.

The concepts ad practice of software project management cannot be a priori transferred to the web management domain due to a whole range of specific characteristics. The most prominent features of web projects are multidisciplinary and working in a small team.

KEYWORD

Web management refers to all of the activities included in the process of posting and maintaining a website on the World Wide Web.

Being a web project manager means managing a small but complex team of diverse experts of various competencies, realizing all major project tasks in sub-groups simultaneously. This implies that a web project manager must invest more communication effort to coordinate and lead the development of such a project well and minimize conflicts and problems, for sub-groups often develop components of similar design, structure, and functionality but from various aspects in relation to the customer.

The success of a web project also depends on the ability of all members to function as a team. The manager must understand each individual function and contribution of each member of the web project team in order to achieve more productive operations.

Web teams consist of young people with about two years of experience, so they are often inclined to use the most recent technologies and development environment without previous consideration of their advantages and disadvantages and without previously determined updating and modifying policies.

On the other hand, the web team manager must remain continuously attentive to customers' opinions and expectations and incorporate them into the web project. The reason for this lies in highly volatile customers' demands that are more often than not contrary to the company's interests or the application's functionality, so that it is essential for the manager to feel and recognize it.

When developing web projects, it is very difficult to predefine the potential buyers and the site's target groups, and specify all their expectations in advance. Moreover, the company is only a click away from losing a prospect or even a loyal customer.

Attempts at attracting new clients and keeping the existing ones, in most cases, result in changing site appearance in order to follow the web design fashion trends (Pressman & Lowe, 2009).

In view of this fact, the manager should avoid coding these site segments and thus prevent disrupting the site's functionality due to frequent changes in appearance.

Web sites are characterized by being developed over a short period, between 3 and 6 months. This feature of web sites stems from continuous developments in the web and technologies, but also the pace of change of the conditions in e-business and clients' demands.

This further means that the design stage of corporate web sites is hard to delineate from the maintenance fight. Due to the fact that company sites are subject to constant evolution, it is very important for the manager of such a project to assess which web engineering model would be the most appropriate for development.

Modern-day web applications are prone to agile models, which produce the prototype, i.e., the first 'draft' of the application, very quickly. A web application manager should also emphasize using as broad a range of tools as possible – for request management, planning, design, implementation, risk management, etc., while still ensuring to keep the development process is independent of the tools.

KEYWORD

Risk management is the process of identifying, assessing and controlling financial, legal, strategic and security risks to an organization's capital and earnings.

Software development experts are disinclined to maintain documentation, which is even more present in programmers due to tight deadlines so that it is also necessary to introduce special tools to this end. However, the significance of documenting frequent site changes is invaluable.

One of the most significant performance indicators of a web application is its usability, so the existence of a unified logic for using the application is essential, as well as simplicity of learning, user error minimization, downloads speed, ease of search, and finally, the user's positive personal experience – or individual perception – once the site use is completed.

The web project manager must have adequate information on the usability of the web project for clients and introduce user testing in the early stages, i.e., initial project prototypes. This testing comes down to defining a representative sample of future application users, establishing tasks to be completed in interaction with the application, and monitoring this process to spot the users' problems in working with the application. One of the leading metrics, i.e., performance indicators in assessing the quality of a web site, is the scalability of the application, meaning that the project manager must also take into consideration this feature of the application so as to prevent huge tangible and intangible losses caused by the growth in the number of users that the application cannot serve.

Although web applications are characterized by rapid development over a very short time and an inexact user group, it is easy to infer that the total development and maintenance costs, and the quality of the application under development, are hard to foresee.

The project manager, therefore, has a very important and responsible task – to apply one of the quality assessment web models, such as the web quality model, goal question metric model, etc.) From the initial development stages.

Did you Know?

Agile approaches increasingly require tools, e.g., for requirements management, planning, design/implementation, test planning and implementation, and error handling as well as continuous configuration management.

7.3. MANAGING THE DEVELOPMENT PROCESS OF A WEB APPLICATION

7.3.1. Deploying the Tools

Web applications are necessarily developed using a very flexible approach, characterized by a high degree of reusability, agile process methods, close customer contact, and a large number of intermediate products.

However, with regard to the tools used and the (intermediate) results produced, one can also observe a transition from the document-driven approach in traditional (rigid) software development towards a highly tool-supported approach in agile development projects (Orr, 2002).

Agile approaches increasingly require tools, e.g., for requirements management, planning, design/implementation, test planning and implementation, and error handling as well as continuous configuration management. This applies in particular to young and inexperienced developers since they may easily lose their grip on the project, especially if it is highly iterative.

In one of the few studies that explicitly deal with management problems in web projects, Cutter Consortium (2000) suggests that "...iterations can easily become ad-hoc developments without tools for progress measurement, change management, and results review... [and]... careful monitoring of the requirements both by the developer and the customer."

The same source mentions that Web projects, in particular, have to be handled based on a documented plan, and that extensive and careful testing is unavoidable, even if the project already suffers from delays. These tools must interact well (or ideally be integrated) to ensure that a development project's efficiency improves (see the Eclipse project at http://www.eclipse.org for an example).

However, care should be taken to ensure that the development process is independent from these tools and technologies (McDonald & Welland, 2001a). Since the technologies available to develop Web applications change rapidly, and unpredictably, the development process should be clearly separated from implementation tools and languages.

In many cases, when moving to an agile approach, people forget that the availability of these tools is only one side of the coin; handling them has to be learned and practiced, too. The time required for such learning processes frequently is not planned for in short Web projects, or their cost cannot be justified.

KEYWORD

PHProjekt is a free groupware and project management web application written in PHP.

Since the developers of Web projects are typically inexperienced, individual "autodidactic" learning of agile methods and the required tools could, in fact, lead to a situation where everything subjectively unimportant is omitted while hacking makes its entrance (Beck & McBreen, 2002).

7.3.1.1. Tools for Web Project Management

Since Web developers are especially familiar with the Web, Web-based tools are ideally suited for Web project management. Web-based project management tools, such as PHProjekt (http://www.PHProjekt.com), allow handling traditional project management (TPM) tasks, such as time recording, maintaining a diary, archiving and versioning result documents, logging, blackboards, chat rooms, e-mail distribution, etc., to support the Web team's communication.

Many of these tools are even free for personal and educational use. In addition, such tools facilitate communication and collaboration beyond local boundaries, which frequently occur in Web projects. Project Management Institute (1999) gives an overview of project management tools, including Web-based tools.

7.3.1.2. Tools for Configuration Management

A configuration management system (Dart, 2000) is an important tool to support an orderly project process. In Web engineering, configuration management is used mainly for the following tasks due to the short iteration cycles:

- Managing versions of the source code and the application content, and regulating access to the content;
- Creating configurations, both for the source code and the application content, to establish an orderly release policy;
- Managing change requests and handling errors and defects;
- Controlling document state to monitor project progress.

Creating variants is less common in Web engineering. If variants are created (by branching in the development tree), then the reason is often just to complete a customer version due to the short iteration cycles while other team members are working on product progress along a second branch.

KEYWORD

Configuration Management is the process of maintaining systems, such as computer hardware and software, in a desired state.

Since many Web projects start small and then successively grow, it is important to use configuration management systems from the very start of the project, even if the project would then seem "too small" for tool-supported configuration management. Changing to configuration management later on would be costly and time-consuming.

Moreover, the evolutionary history cannot be tracked unless one uses a configuration management tool from the start of the project. When a Web project is broken down into many small subprojects and their results have to be consolidated for each (intermediate) product, a configuration management tool will quickly become an indispensable part of the Web application development project (Baskerville & Levine, 2001).

Configuration management allows specifying who may change what and when, and it lets one control these changes. Especially in Web engineering, components of an application are often created by people less experienced in software engineering.

They often create a large number of versions of one single component or document, quickly losing track of the purposes of each of these versions or whether a version is still up-to-date. This situation causes the number of documents in Web projects to grow dramatically, particularly because documents with multimedia content (so-called assets, comprising, e.g., music clips or videos) require a lot of memory. Many tools available to manage configurations of software being developed (e.g., Visual Source Safe, http://msdn.microsoft.com/ssafe; Subversion, http://www.subversion.com; Clear

Case, http://www.rational.com/products/clearcase) have difficulties in processing assets (large memory demand) and identifying version differences (binary format).

Some configuration tools may not even be able to process such assets due to the data demand. This is probably the reason why many configuration management tools for multimedia are still being developed individually (Wallner, 2001).

7.3.2. Measuring Progress

When developing Web applications, often just two documents are created (McDonald & Welland, 2001a). The first document is the system specification, containing the results from the requirements analysis and design decisions. The second "document" is the finished Web application.

This Web application is normally created in a quick sequence of intermediate results by means of highly iterative and evolutionary prototyping. Sharma (2001) suggests that the iteration steps should be as small as possible and have clearly defined functionality.

Each of these steps should be followed by a review, ideally involving the customer. This approach is identical to rapid application development (RAD), a technique that has been well known and frequently practiced in traditional software development for almost 20 years.

KEYWORD

Assets are specific items that directly provide a financial benefit or establish ownership of a financial benefit.

The development of Web applications is characterized by the fact that their requirements generally cannot be estimated beforehand, which means that project size and cost cannot be anticipated either (Reifer, 2002).

In addition, the usual high pressure with regard to a defined and very short delivery deadline means that "the quality of a fixed-time product should be estimated rather than the costs for a well-specified system" (Pressman, 1998).

The difficulties in anticipating these factors and the subsequent progress control of Web projects have been summarized by D. Reifer and used to develop a Web-specific project metric. This metric considers the use of Web-specific components and a large amount of reuse in the following manner.

Analogous to "software objects" of the COCOMO II model (Boehm et al., 2000), Reifer defines so-called "Web objects," enabling the use of COCOMO-like object points for Web components (Reifer, 2002), where the functional links have to be adapted considerably (*see* Reifer, 2002 for details; and Olsina et al., 2005 for an overview of other Web metrics).

Of course, clearly defined counting guidelines for Web objects are important to obtain meaningful estimates, similar to any other metric. However, this doesn't solve the main problem that development-related design components are counted, i.e., that there is more input on the developer side and less on the customer side. Counting is a nice method to measure progress. But it doesn't answer the question of whether or not the degree of objective coverage can be improved.

Remember

The major objectives of project management that must be met are cost, performance, time goals while in parallel it must control or maintains the purpose of the project at the defined level.

7.3.3. Project Risks

7.3.3.1. Risks in Software Development

A risk is the possibility of an activity causing loss or damage. However, we speak of risk only if the consequences are uncertain. This means that a risk represents a potential problem (Thayer & Fairley, 1997). There is no such thing as a project without risks (and problems resulting from them).

"If a project is successful, then it is not successful because there were no risks and problems, but because risks and problems have been handled successfully" (Rook, 1986). Each risk also represents an economic chance. A shorter development cycle can translate into a desirable competitive edge for a product's time-to-market.

The venture of using a new technology can open up additional market segments. For example, the use of the .NET platform allows the deployment to Microsoft-based mobile phones as possible target devices. The most important risks in software development have been identified and updated regularly by B. Boehm, one of the pioneers in the field of risk management in software engineering, since the 1980s.

The second new risk element of the 1990s represents the use of legacy software, i.e., the use of historically grown software systems. In the 1980s, it was common to think that this problem could be solved by re-implementation, which turned out to be wrong.

Especially in the development of Web applications, many legacy systems have to be embedded, such as data management/storage systems. For example, the author supervised a project for a large metal spare parts supplier who wanted to offer their services on the Internet.

Within this project, a COBOL environment with a hierarchical database as the primary information system had to be embedded into the Web application to be built (by use of wrapper technologies). Neither did the company want to replace its existing database system, nor was it feasible because the entire corporate operation depended on this database, as the company committed to extremely short delivery times as its major trademark.

7.3.3.2. Specific Risks in Web Engineering

In Web engineering, the main reasons for delays or total failure of Web projects are identical to the main risks listed by B. Boehm. Projects fail primarily due to bad communication between the Web project team and the customer, i.e., personal deficits.

The second important reason is a poor understanding of the development processes for a Web application (McDonald & Welland, 2001a). J. Nielsen, the "guru of Web page usability," mentions the following top-ten list of risks in a Web project, especially addressing web project management (Nielsen, 1997b):

- **Unclear Definition of Objectives:** Many web applications are created without clearly explaining the purpose of the application to the developers. A company can address totally different customer objectives with a Web application; a service application with a help desk meets totally different tasks than an online catalog with an ordering function.

It is important to clearly specify the objectives and how customers can profit from a Web application and to explain these objectives to everybody on the team. McDonald & Welland (2001a) mentions poor objectives research and requirements analysis as the main reasons for the immaturity of current development processes for Web applications.

- **Wrong Target Audience:** Many web applications are heavily oriented to the wishes of corporate management (mission statements, manager profiles, etc.) while failing to address the application's target group.
- **Development-Oriented Page Structure:** The easiest way for developers to create content is by following the contractor's organizational chart. Once this structure has been applied to an application, it is frequently no longer

KEYWORD

COBOL is a compiled English-like computer programming language designed for business use.

possible to follow a customer-oriented operation. The application will be focused on the company rather than on the users.

- **Lacking Consistency Due to Outsourcing:** If the development of different Web applications of the same company (or parts of a larger Web application) is outsourced to different external companies, there is a high risk that the individuality of these external companies will be strongly reflect in the applications, especially in the contents and navigation aids.

KEYWORD

Hypermedia is a nonlinear medium of information that includes graphics, audio, video, plain text and hyperlinks.

Each of these companies will introduce its profile and try to distinguish itself from its competitors, leading to a botched-up job with regard to the look and feel and the operation of the application.

Pressman (2000b) suggests defining the target audience, its interest in the product, and the general design either internally or by one single company functioning as a coordinator. In addition, regular reviews of the interim products are necessary to ensure that inconsistencies between application parts can be identified early and removed.

- **Lacking Budget for Maintenance:** While traditional software development projects estimate 10% to 15% for annual maintenance (Mayr, 2005), the maintenance cost for Web applications is much higher due to their quickly aging contents and rapidly changing technologies.

Nielsen (1997b) recommends estimating at least 50% of the development cost (100% is more appropriate) annually for maintenance.

- **Content Recycling:** Many try to extract content for Web applications from traditional document sources. It is often overlooked that these media are generally designed to be read and looked at linearly (from front to back). In contrast, the Web lives on the non-linearity of the hypermedia structure and its linking.

The possibilities offered by a non-linear media structure are not utilized because many application and business experts have grown up on purely linear content (printed books, newspaper articles), and they have been educated to create linear content for traditional media. The rethinking process has been slow in this field.

- **Poor Linking:** Recycling linear content leads to the problem that links are often added "artificially," which can be detrimental rather than beneficial (e.g. converting printed manuals into online help systems).

In addition, many links point to higher-order pages rather than pointing to specific content. It is then up to the user to find the desired content from the general starting point and to have the patience to do this.

- **Mixing Internet and Intranet:** While an Internet presence represents a company to the outside, thus transporting corporate culture, PR ideas, etc., in addition to information, to potential court users, an intranet serves to efficiently support the work of an exactly defined user group – the company's staff.

For this reason, the efficiency of Web applications in an intranet should clearly be given preference over PR and (exaggerated) esthetics. Within the intranet, productivity is the goal, and the users are assumed to be loyal.

This means that Internet and intranet applications have to be clearly separated. When developing a Web application, the developers need to know in advance whether it is created for the Internet or an intranet.

- **Confusing Marketing Research and Usability Research:** While marketing research assesses users' wishes, usability research aims to find out how users handle a Web application and what problems they have.

Marketing research can never discover that a Web application's functionality is desirable, but not attractive because it is hard to use. Confusing the two fields of research can lead to wrong assumptions, similar to what happened to some car suppliers who, at the end of the 1990s, cut down on complaint hotlines for cost reasons to then happily notice a clear drop in complaint cases per product.

- **Underestimating the Strategic Significance of the Web:** Every company has taken web presence for granted. In the long term, ignoring this communication channel will lead to significant competitive disadvantages.

However, many companies have overestimated the significance of the Web (cf. the "dotcom crash") and have then made the mistake of developing a Web aversion, missing the bus in the long term.

KEYWORD

Marketing research is the systematic gathering, recording, and analysis of qualitative and quantitative data about issues relating to marketing products and services.

7.3.4. Risk Management

Risk management means proactively considering that there is a certain probability that problems may occur in a project. This is done by estimating the probability, analyzing the impact of potential problems, and preparing suitable problem solutions in advance (Bennatan, 2000). In this way, software development "without surprises" is made possible.

Both the risk management tasks and the processes are the same in Web engineering and other software development fields. The only difference lies in the kind of risks to be handled. We will thus not discuss each step involved in risk management in detail and instead refer our readers to (Mayr, 2005).

Risk management can be thought of as a form of insurance that covers a problem by immediately providing a solution as soon as the problem arises. In many cases, a problem that has been analyzed and caught in time is much easier and cheaper to solve than a problem that turns up unexpectedly.

KEYWORD

Cost–benefit analysis is a systematic approach to estimating the strengths and weaknesses of alternatives.

Risk management doesn't provide general recipes for all kinds of cases. However, the literature points to the fact that groups perform much better than individuals while working on risk management activities (Gemmer, 1997).

A risk-driven method, e.g., a spiral model, allows the group to optimally integrate risk management into the project development process. Though risk management doesn't come for free, it should be cost-efficient, i.e., its benefits should outweigh its costs.

However, since risk management is supposed to avoid problems, good risk management can face the situation of justifying the costs spent for analyzing problems that never occurred. For this reason, a sound cost-benefit analysis is indispensable to justify risk management activities (Pressman, 2005).

7.4. AGILE VS. TRADITIONAL WEB PROJECT MANAGEMENT

The agile approach to management contains several well-known methods: Scrum, DSDM (Dynamic Systems Development Methodology), Extreme Programming, etc. Applying these may result in web solutions within the defined triple program limitations, i.e., within foreseen deadlines, with a planned budget and quality.

These are iterative methods, where the delivery time of a single iteration (prototype) is almost on a weekly basis so that it is suitable for project of independent, frequently changing project requirements and requests, including the projects of building a company's corporate web site.

The fundamental difference between the traditional and agile approaches to project management is the essentially different angles of viewing the project. The basic principle in the traditional approach to management is that the volume of work defined by the project is invariable, whereas time and budget are the project's fluctuating categories, and the quality of the solution depends on the possibilities.

Applying this principle has resulted in high losses for companies caused by delays in project activities and frequently exceeded budgets. The agile approach presents the categories of the completion time of individual iteration and completion of the entire project as a fixed category.

Two more fixed categories are the delivery price and the solution's defined quality level. The sole changeable category in agile project management (APM) is the volume of work, which can be reduced by not completing activities assessed as a lower priority.

The agile approach is based on the principle of developing prototypes and involving the users in testing these. Developing traditional software products was managed by traditional methods, i.e., by plan-driven development. Due to rapid development and emergence of highly complex web applications revealed numerous shortcomings in relation to the described specifics of web projects.

The newly arisen conditions saw a more intensive utilization of the new agile approach to development management. In a very short time, the agile management approach gained popularity compared to traditional management methods.

However, in time, the practice has shown that using this method does not always produce a positive outcome in a web project development, thus leading to a conclusion that neither of the methods warrants absolute dominance in practice (Magdaleno, 2010).

Such an overview in literature can also be corroborated by the fact that many great IT companies worldwide are bound to have used some of the approaches to corporate web site development

KEYWORD

Agile project management is an iterative approach to managing software development projects that focuses on continuous releases and incorporating customer feedback with every iteration.

management, but there is virtually no written record on how large and successful IT companies choose methods for managing their successful web projects.

The authors of this chapter agree with prominent authors dealing with this issue that the combination of these two approaches to IT project management is necessary (Hayata & Jianchao, 2011), as well as a tie inevitable methodological tenet that would point the manner and extent of mixing them in managing the development of a particular project.

KEYWORD

Extreme project management is one of the modern approaches to project management in software industry.

In his book, Effective Project Management: Traditional, Agile, and Extreme Methods, Wysocki based his IT project management model generally on the assumption that the characteristics of an IT project determine the method of managing it.

He based this model on two variables: aims and solutions, which can be clear and complete or unclear and incomplete. His model, termed "project landscape," generates four different IT project management methods: TPM, APM, extreme project management (xPM), and Emertxe project management (MPx).

In our opinion, this approach is a good springboard for developing a model related to web projects exclusively, for the category of IT projects included into this model is too diverse despite the fact that web projects are characterized by a whole range of specific characteristics, systematized in the first section of the chapter.

Extending this model, and including other important parameters of web projects, as a sub-category of IT projects, would produce a more precise and comprehensive multicriteria model. Within the first stage of our research, we identified the key area that could serve as a source in the following stage for identifying the key indicators that should be included in the future model of choosing a web project management method.

Having studied the literature and conducted interviews in leading Serbian IT companies, the first research stage resulted in differentiating three key areas:

- The specifics of the IT company, its web teams and technologies used in developing;
- The specifics of the client the project is developed for; and
- The specifics of the project itself – the type and main characteristics of the application developed for the user.

In our opinion, there is a high correlation between the above areas and the choice of the appropriate web project management method, i.e., every project is characterized by a set of different specific features in all three areas, so that the mix of the two key methods will also be unique to each particular project.

Furthermore, this means that the practice will produce a set of newly induced management methods based on two key methods. Such a personalized approach to web project management would reduce the percentage of web projects that failed due to inappropriate management.

7.5. WEB-BASED PROJECT MANAGEMENT SYSTEMS (WPMS)

Web based project management systems (WPMS) focus on tools and services that make it easier to manage AEC projects. The essence of collaboration software is to develop a process whereby documents are all electronic, thus enabling them to be located at a secure central location that can be accessed by those to who access rights have been given while maintaining business processes, supply chain relationships, and organizational hierarchies (Figure 7.2).

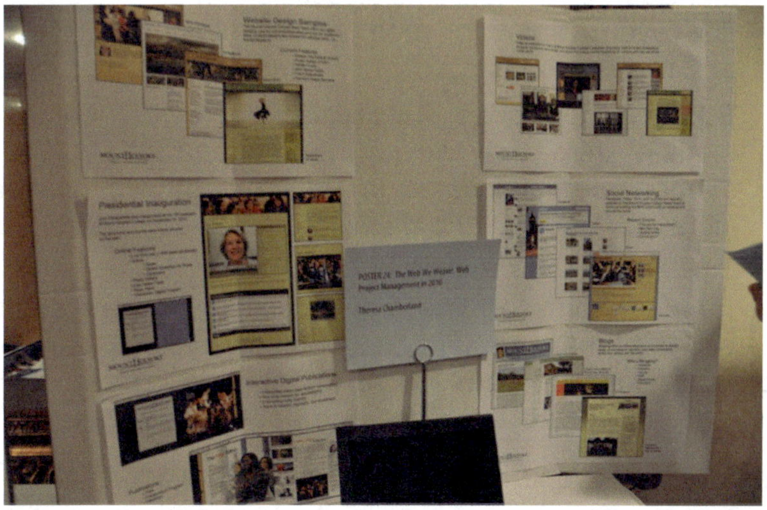

Figure 7.2. *Web-based project management.*

Source: Image by Flickr.

Online project management provides an instant, on-demand, secure online solution for every team member to communicate, share documents and collaborate using a standard web browser. WPMS are an out-sourced Internet-based project information and workflow management service for the design, engineering, and construction industry.

It provides specialized tools for all the individuals involved in the building process and enables construction projects to be completed under budget and ahead of schedule. This service focuses on providing project teams with rapid, secure, and easy access to information.

It promotes the concept of 'partnering' – enabling project owners, planners, and architects to collaborate and jointly determine how best to achieve the project's goals. To implement effective partnering, all project players must remain in regular contact with each other and have access to the same data.

To ensure effective coordination of the numerous partners that make up the project team, it is critical to get everyone communicating as quickly and efficiently as possible.

KEYWORD

Team communication refers to the interactions colleagues share with each other.

- **Document Management:** Sharing or viewing multiple file formats online, marking up the documents, downloading and uploading multiple documents, document search or full text search, backup facilities, keeping a document revision history, and track who accesses what files.
- **Team Communication (Project Collaboration and Management):** Real time discussion group, project calendar and event planning, team communication (project email or SMS messaging).
- **Business Process Automation:** Browser compatibility, plotting, third-party viewer, MAC support, PDA, and WAP support, server located in a secure data center, firewall installed, User ID and password required, different access levels, virus protection.

The heart of some on line project management systems is a secure document management and workflow system that stores all project documents and forms. The information repository can be updated daily to ensure everyone can access current information.

It enables everyone in the project team to work from the same page, improving productivity. It helps to accelerate time to-market, reduce cost, and increase revenues and to minimize rework due to communications errors.

With a minimal investment in Internet technology and personnel, WPMS provides the tools for instant information access anytime and anywhere; collaborative software offers any kind of information services (consult, procure, maintain, modify, etc.) throughout the life cycle of the project.

7.5.1. Advantages of WPMS

The adoption and benefits gained in using WPMS within the AEC industry have been studied by Price Waterhouse Coopers and many real and tangible benefits currently being experienced by early adopters have been found (Price Waterhouse Coopers, 2002).

In this part, it's said that overall, the use of these tools within the industry; is in its infancy, with architects, engineers, and general contractors leading the way. Owners, developers, and subcontractors currently seem to be slower in their adoption, in part due to limited exposure to the use of these tools and infrastructure issues.

They believe that the benefits currently being realized by early adopters cover only a limited range of the services that WPMS can potentially offer; today, these benefits center around:

- Better communication. WPMS improves project progress communication, and alignment of business processes increases transparency as barriers to communication are removed; Collaborative systems reduce the amount of re-work by storing not just information but the knowledge that derived it.
- Reduction of costs and wasted time. Printing and postage costs and document administration are reduced as all documents are stored centrally.
- Improvement of project control. All actions are recorded to be audited and monitored.
- Better access to information and reduced response time for RFI (Requests for Information), CO (Change Orders), and specifications clarification.
- Shorten the project life cycle. The fast dissemination of information shortens consultation cycles and speeds up decision making. When you send an electronic document to a website, it is immediately available for viewing; likewise, written feedback is available without delay.
- Improvement of connectivity. The Potential for interoperability with business applications provides a near-term project-based perspective.

KEYWORD

Collaborative System is an information system used to facilitate efficient sharing of data, documents, files, information, and knowledge between teams and employees in an organization.

- Reduction of risk and potential errors. The latest information is always available as soon as it is published, minimizing the risk of working on old information.

These benefits have far-reaching implications for construction projects. By improving project progress communication, all team members are kept informed of issues in a timely manner, project schedules are distributed faster, and consequently, less overlapping and/or no show of workers would occur.

If the cycle-time taken to turn around an RFI/CO is shortened, this could directly impact the project's length: with fewer delays and quicker response times, the project's life cycle can be shortened. Shortening the life cycle of construction brings benefits such as reduced expenditures in person-hours, equipment rentals, project site office costs, and security costs. It allows the project team to begin working on new revenue-generating projects.

KEYWORD

Threat is a communication of intent to inflict harm or loss on another person.

Finally, tenants can occupy the site earlier by completing the project sooner, and owners/developers can enjoy earlier rental/lease revenue. As the AEC industry embraces these tools, all participants will progressively realize additional benefits.

It's foreseen that as understanding of client needs and adoption increases, vendors will develop product offerings to meet the needs of all industry players; in turn, these will increase the overall usage of online project collaboration tools. It's believed that the AEC industry will open itself up and adopt the changes brought about by developing online collaboration tools.

7.5.2. Limitations of WPMS

There are also drawbacks when an organization decides to work using WPMS:

- **Security:** The possibility of sharing information in a WPMS demands security measures. The issue of trust is a major issue in setting up such a WPMS – some clients would be completely trustworthy, while others would need to be checked all the time. There is definitely a need to ensure that people are encouraged to see this technology as a benefit rather than a threat.
- **Infrastructure and Difficult Internet Access:** Companies need to have the infrastructure necessary to support them (i.e., network systems, hardware, etc.). Most companies

don't have this infrastructure and don't want to change their organizations. Moreover, there is mostly no Internet access on site.

- **Need for Training:** Employees must be familiar with technological solutions; otherwise, they need to be trained. Some employees are not keen on using new technologies and think they will need too much time to learn and understand them.

7.6. UTILIZATION OF WPMS IN THE CONSTRUCTION INDUSTRY

The AEC industry is in the early days of adopting these online collaboration tools; however, early adopters already realize some of the benefits to be gained (Price Waterhouse Coopers, 2002).

In general, architects, engineers, and general contractors are adopting WPMS and understand the benefits to be gained. Subcontractors are the least likely users of online tools, and although keen to try this technology, owners, and developers are hesitant to adopt it at this stage.

Further reasons for the adoption and non-adoption of online tools are:

- Architects and engineers are most likely to use online project collaboration tools as they:
  - have the infrastructure necessary to support them (i.e., network systems, hardware, etc.);
  - have employees familiar with technological solutions such as computer-aided design (CAD).
- General contractors are also keen adopters of these tools; some of the reasons are that they:
  - have seen some of the associated benefits through demonstrations and marketing efforts;
  - have been mandated to utilize a specific tool by an owner/developer or architect, felt much of the communication frustrations, and could foresee that these tools would help to alleviate this burden;
  - have the infrastructure necessary to support the tools.
- Owners and developers had mixed responses regarding the adoption of online tools. Some were early adopters,

KEYWORD

Computer-aided design is the use of computers to aid in the creation, modification, analysis, or optimization of a design.

whereas others were not. Reasons for their positions include adoption driven by marketing and advertising campaigns – resistance attributed to the lack of a critical mass of players within the industry currently using the tools.

- Subcontractors have to date been the most resistant to adopting these tools. Those using them were doing so because they – have been approached to be part of a project team using a particular tool – have seen advertising/ marketing efforts – believed that this was how work would evolve in the future.

TIPS

Many web-based services have launched in the construction industry over the last eight years, in line with similar trends across all industries

Collectively, reasons for resistance centered on the lack of exposure and education about these tools within the industry. As evidenced by the research, the drivers to adoption in the AEC industry are less about understanding the benefits and more about perceived benefits, client recommendations, and awareness brought on by marketing campaigns.

7.7. TYPES OF WEB-BASED SOFTWARE FOR THE CONSTRUCTION INDUSTRY

Over the previous eight years, a large number of web-based services have been introduced in the construction sector, following general industry trends. Several of these portals failed quickly because of the competitive nature of the sector in which they operate and the lack of established business models for effective systems. These services generally fall into four categories:

- Information portals;
- Enterprise portals;
- Electronic marketplaces; and
- Web based project management systems (WPMS)/ extranets.

7.7.1. Information Portals

A portal is a website designed with a particular audience and community in mind. It offers highly tailored content aggregation, delivery of audience-relevant information, collaboration, community services, and access to services and apps for the target audience.

The following criteria, known as the "four C's," should be met by a portal: Connection to the internet resources via search engines, online stores, and other tools; Content in the form of suitable news, entertainment, and educational materials for interested users; Commerce involving access to electronic shopping and other commercial activity; Communities of interest established by ground rules and tools that allow participants to engage.

The demand for portal technology evolved initially as a result of the necessity to assist users in accessing the information on the open Internet. Very soon after, as intranets gained popularity and staff members looked for a way to organize information inside the boundaries of the company, the same requirement started to emerge inside of companies.

Remember

If a project is successful, then it is not successful because there were no risks and problems, but because risks and problems have been handled successfully.

Since then, the range and capabilities of portal technology have expanded to a second generation of vertical portals. These solutions concentrated on indexing and arranging particular sorts of information and application services, mostly for corporate use.

Today, third-generation portal technology allows for integrating a huge variety of business data and applications from both inside and outside the company. These e-business portal technologies are able to give a common framework of services upon which to create vertical portals.

Information portals are intended for general use and serve as the primary source of information. They provide categorized connections to other websites but do not allow for business-to-business transactions, but they may be used to identify commercial partners. Most of the information portals that are currently in use are built using manufactured goods. They frequently copy paper-based catalogs, sometimes to the point where they scan them in order to deliver their service. The advantage of this strategy is somewhat minimal; the only improvement over a paper system (assumed that the speed of information access is roughly equivalent) is that modifications are immediately visible to all users.

7.7.2. Enterprise Portals

Enterprise portals focus on business operations and provide information and transaction functionality for all parties involved in a single firm. Project management tools may also be accessible, particularly in enterprise portals tied to the AEC industry. This type of website may be built on the Internet, an Intranet, an Extranet, or a mix of these platforms.

7.7.3. Electronic Marketplaces

A website that offers transaction capability between two or more companies is known as an electronic marketplace. Providing extra features like managing product catalogs, auctions, reverse auctions, and others is typical. Again, AEC-related e-marketplaces may offer project management.

The term "electronic business" refers to the electronic exchange of tangible goods as well as intangibles like information, as well as all the trading processes like online ordering, payment, and delivery support, as well as the electronic delivery of services like online after-sales support or legal advice.

KEYWORD

Electronic commerce is the activity of electronically buying or selling of products on online services or over the Internet.

It also refers to electronic support for corporate collaboration, such as collaborative design. Electronic commerce is a subset of e-business that is concentrated on e-procurement, e-buying, e-payment, etc. and represents 'punctual' operations with a short duration.

Few portals allow for the selection of products based on their performance attributes, whereas some portals enable e-commerce to purchase particular products. In order to expand these services, portals frequently include a specific group of relevant information services, such as access to standards papers, industry news feeds, and databases of certain industry professionals.

These websites are frequently criticized for being underdeveloped. This is frequently true, not just for their primary informational content (i.e., their manufactured products) but more so for their related services, which typically only contain a small percentage of the information available to the industry.

7.7.4. Web-Based Project Management Systems/Extranet

Web-based project management systems are web-based programs made for managing and storing project data. Applications for project collaboration simply give different groups of people, such as clients, engineers, and architects, regulated access to and automated dissemination of information.

The purpose of collaboration has always been the same: to do tasks more effectively, quickly, and affordably by combining various resources and utilizing their combined skills and knowledge.

Effective teamwork increases output, streamlines and optimizes decision-making, and assists in capturing priceless intellectual property (Ball, 2004).

Systems are created to enhance collaboration between the teams working on a project, lowering risks and assisting in ensuring that the project is finished on schedule. All project participants utilize them to access, read, print, and edit materials in accordance with permissions established by the project administrator.

They serve as a repository for all project-related papers, drawings, and correspondence. There are two types of solutions: ASP (software located outside the company and rented out) and Enterprise (billed by license fees and related maintenance).

TIPS

It's believed that the AEC industry will open itself up and adopt the changes brought about by the development of online collaboration tools.

Application service providers (ASPs) are third-party organizations that administer and deliver software-based services and solutions to clients through a wide area network from a centralized data center. In essence, ASPs are a way for companies to outsource some or almost all the aspects of their information technology (IT) needs.

BIW and ProjectNet are the market leaders relative to project extranets; they have the largest number of users, and their system is highly regarded. Business Collaborator and BIW are the WPMS that clients are most satisfied with, and their adaptability offers sophisticated functionalities. What is interesting about the different offerings is that their functionality appears to be converging.

BIW's application now includes flexible functionality to suit individual client business processes; Business Collaborator is developing a more rigid "project extranet" product from its flexible tool kit, etc. Build Online's ability to win major contracts with excellent clients, together with its track record of acquisitions, positions the business well.

SUMMARY

- **Definition of Project Management:** This part of the chapter summarizes project management's definitions, challenges, and limitations. Types of web-based software for the construction industry have also been explained. The different types are information portals, enterprise portals, electronic marketplaces, and web-based project management system.
- **The Specifics of Web Projects:** The middle of the chapter explains the Specifics of Web Projects—the Agile Vs. Traditional Web Project Management. The Web Based Project Management System is explained in brief in this section, along with the Advantages and Limitations of WPMS.
- **Utilization of WPMS in the Construction Industry:** The end of the chapter summarizes the utilization of WPMS in the Construction Industry. It also educates about the management of the development process of a Web Application. They deploy the tools, measure progress, project risks, and risk management.

REVIEW QUESTIONS

1. Define project management?
2. What are the challenges in project management?
3. What are the limitations of project management?
4. Explain information portals and enterprise portals?
5. What do you understand about the electronic marketplace?
6. Explain web-based project management system?
7. What are the advantages and limitations of web based project management system?
8. What do you mean by risk management?

MULTIPLE CHOICE QUESTIONS

1. Which of the following is not a project management goal?

a. Keeping overall costs within budget
b. Delivering the software to the customer at the agreed time
c. Maintaining a happy and well-functioning development team
d. Avoiding customer complaints

2. Which of the following is not considered as a risk in Project Management?

a. Specification delays
b. Product competition

c. Testing
d. Staff turnover

3. **The process each manager follows during the life of a project is known as –**
   a. Project management
   b. Manager life cycle
   c. Project management life cycle
   d. All of the above
4. **Quality planning is the process of developing a quality plan for**
   a. Team
   b. Project
   c. Customers
   d. Project manager
5. **Which of the following is an incorrect activity for the configuration management of a software system?**
   a. Internship management
   b. Change management
   c. Version management
   d. System management

Answers to Multiple Choice Questions

1. (d) 2. (c) 3. (c) 4. (b) 5. (a)

REFERENCES

1. Aadamsoo, A. M., (2010). *Web Based Project Management System.* core.ac.uk. University of Applied Sciences. Available at: https://core.ac.uk/download/pdf/38008713.pdf (accessed on 04 March 2023).
2. Izang, A. A., et al., (2016). A web-based project management system. publication.babcock.edu.ng. *International Journal of Advanced Research in Computer Science and Software Engineering.* Available at: https://www.academia.edu/25086781/A_Web_Based_Project_Management_System (accessed on 04 March 2023).
3. Karatzas, G., (2010). *Web-based Project Management.* docplayer.net. University of East Anglia. Available at: https://docplayer.net/11192919-Web-based-project-management.html (accessed on 04 March 2023).
4. Karatzas, G., (2014). *Web-Based Project Management.* Academia.edu. University of East Anglia. Available at: https://www.academia.edu/1961546/Web_based_Project_Management (accessed on 04 March 2023).

5. *Web Based Project Management Systems,* (n.d). upcommons.upc.edu. UPC Universitat politècnica. Available at: https://upcommons.upc.edu/bitstream/handle/2117/93472/05Nfm05de12.pdf?sequence=5 (accessed on 04 March 2023).

6. Zabierowski, W., Galezowski, G., & Napieralski, A., (2009). *Web-Based Project Management System*. ResearchGate. CADSM. Available at: https://www.researchgate.net/publication/261858984_Web-based_Project_Management_System (accessed on 04 March 2023).

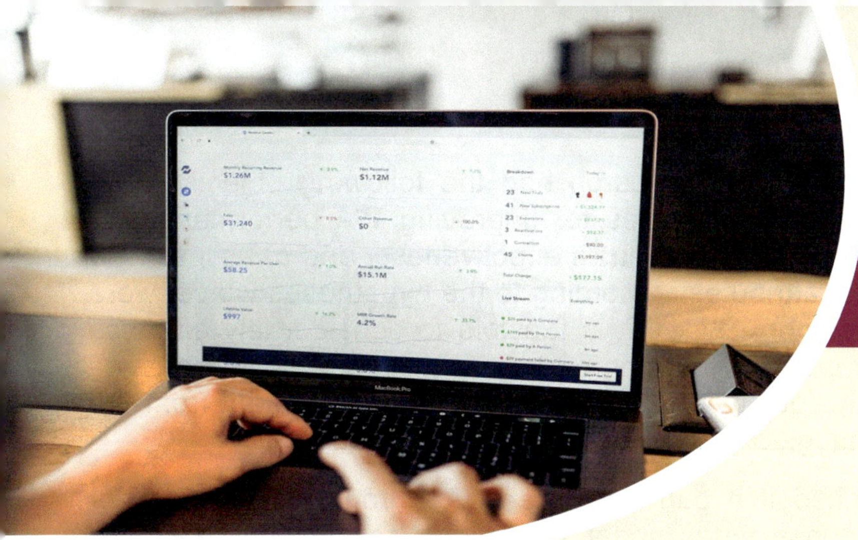

CHAPTER 8

PERFORMANCE OF WEB APPLICATION

UNIT INTRODUCTION

In the previous unit, we discussed about project management definitions, challenges, and limitations. We discussed the types of web-based software for the construction industry, like – information portals, enterprise portals, electronic marketplaces, and web based project management. We also covered the web based project management advantages and limitations in this chapter and furthermore, and we discussed in the previous chapter.

Now in the present unit, we will extend our discussion on performance definitions, characteristics, and system performance. We will discuss the performance evaluation, including system definition and indicators. Including analytical techniques and performance optimization methods, which we will discuss in this chapter.

Web applications (WAs) have proliferated, enabling anyone with only rudimentary IT skills to launch an online business utilizing a free (open source) or commercial WA. Three fundamental elements have contributed to the current prominence of WA performance.

Firstly, the proliferation of broadband Internet connections has altered visitor expectations and their tolerance for waiting for an application to reply, lowering the expected duration to 1 or 2 seconds. The second component is the expanding burden brought on by the steadily rising number of Internet users.

The third factor is the newly proposed usage paradigm by Web 2.0, which states that user content production equals write-intensive WAs. All this has increased the pressure on the performance of web applications. Our research had the following objectives: a) make a thorough analysis of the various techniques for improving WA performance, b) experimentally test, gauge, and assess each technique's effectiveness, and c) assess how different methods affect the WA quality attributes. According to the hypotheses we set were (a) regardless of the application's category (type), it is feasible to considerably enhance performance on the same hardware basis by utilizing even a tiny subset of performance enhancement approaches; and (b) the quality traits of such applications benefit from the use of performance optimization strategies (efficiency, availability, reliability).

The first hypothesis will be verified if it can enhance (WA) throughput by 30% or more while maintaining 90% of response times under 2 seconds and an average CPU use of 70% or less. The second hypothesis will be proven correct if the average CPU consumption is reduced by 10% or more while the throughput is increased by at least 30%. We chose three well-known open source programs from different categories to experimentally test our hypotheses.

The applications that we selected were:

- Joomla content management system (marked APP1);
- PhpBB online community system (APP2); and
- Os commerce e-commerce system (APP3).

We chose these applications because they have been around for a while, they are popular among millions of users every day, and they are the go-to choice for many prosperous web businesses. The performance of WAs can be improved using one of three fundamental strategies. While pre-fetching and caching are well-known techniques from other computing fields, response time and size minimization is a relatively new strategy created by some of the most popular applications on the Internet today. We will highlight some of the most significant work that has been done using these methodologies in this section. Caching is one of the earliest techniques for performance improvement today in various information systems. In the field of web application development, caching has been examined by Na et al. (2006); Khayari et al. (2006); Bahn et al. (2005); Amza et al. (2005); and Sajeev (2009), while Sivasubramanian has examined several caching algorithms in his book (Sivasubramanian, 2007).

Perfecting, or getting ready to transfer data that will likely be requested after the previous request, is another growing area of performance improvement. Domenech evaluated the effectiveness of a number of perfecting methods (Domenech et al., 2006) and developed perfecting algorithms with improved prediction outcomes (Domenech et al., 2007).

Predicting which information will be requested next is one of the essential components of perfecting. Prediction is typically based on the analysis and modeling of user behavior as described by Georghakis (2006) or by extracting usage patterns from web server logs, as has been done by Liu et al. (2007); and Huang et al. (2008). Lam et al. (2006) suggested adding a time component to help decide the ideal moment to perfect web assets.

Learning Objectives

Following the completion of the chapter, the students should be able to understand the following:

- Understand what performance is;
- Understand the performance of web applications;
- Understand what characterizes the performance of web applications;
- Understand the performance evaluation;
- Understand the different analytical techniques;
- Understand the performance optimization methods.

Key Terms

- Performance
- Characterizes
- Evaluation
- Acceleration
- Techniques
- Queuing
- Transmission

8.1. WHAT IS PERFORMANCE?

Depending on the load to be processed, performance measurements are often stated in a system's response time (R), throughput (X), or utilization (U). The time between making a request to a system and getting a response from it is often referred to as the response time.

The throughput and utilization indicate how many requests can be handled per time unit and the percentage of time the system used, respectively.

Assuming a linear relationship between workload and throughput, which is determined by the number of requests fulfilled per time unit, at first glance, we can define the workload by the quantity of requests that are received by the system per unit of time.

KEYWORD

Service-level agreement is a commitment between a service provider and a customer.

If we were to maximize throughput to service as many requests per time unit as possible, then an approach that gets the system as close as feasible to the theoretical maximum capacity would be ideal. However, the response time increases in line with increasing throughput, so it is generally not a good idea to try to optimize throughput for an interactive information system.

As such, reaction time is frequently employed as a performance parameter for Web applications. A typical performance formulation, such as the formulations used in various Web benchmarks, for instance, indicates the maximum throughput defined by the HTTP requests handled within a specific time period, during which a given threshold value for the response time is not surpassed.

This threshold value is known as the service level agreement (SLA), and the throughput value corresponding to this threshold is known as the nominal system capacity. Performance analysis focuses on determining the relationship between performance indicators like response time, throughput, and utilization, workload, and the performance-relevant characteristics of the system under study. Additionally, it aims to identify performance issues or bottlenecks and set performance-improving strategies.

Modeling techniques abstract the performance-relevant properties from a system description and map them to a model, so they are not always dependent on an existent system for analysis. Depending on the complexity of the model, we can also employ analytical procedures or simulations to establish the performance measures.

8.2. PERFORMANCE OF WEB APPLICATIONS

The quality of the architecture is what essentially determines the quality and, consequently, the performance of WAs. The expected or required performance level can be limited or entirely blocked (by acting as a bottleneck) by poorly constructed application architecture components.

Production teams have started to adopt performance risk management in all stages of their lifecycle as a result of the renewed emphasis on the significance of application performance.

TIPS

Web server replication is another technique that does not forward a client request directly to the addressed server but redirects it to a replicate of that server.

According to research conducted by the Aberdeen group (2008), organizations that have implemented performance management using the PACE (Pressures, Actions, Capabilities, Enablers) model has seen improvements in the availability of 106%, response times that are 11.4 times faster, and a problem-solving rate of 85% before their users notice the issue.

However, there are now a lot of WAs in use throughout the world, and as more people use them, performance needs to be improved to reach the intended service levels. There are three basic sources of motivation for performance improvement:

- The desire to increase the number of users or profit;
- Expected and planned peak workload periods; and
- Performance improvement is driven by a business plan or motivated by a genuine or anticipated (projected) performance issue with the aim of assuring availability and effectiveness under an increased workload.

Performance improvement always involves making trade-offs between a variety of competing elements, including spending caps on hardware and labor hours, desirable response times and throughput values, etc. While attempting to optimize a third component, we had to strike a balance between two limiting aspects in our research (throughput)...

As the first limiting element, we have set the average response time for 90% of queries to 2 seconds since this is now the non-written benchmark for most popular WAs on the WWW today. The typical CPU utilization during stress tests is displayed along the Z axis.

According to another widely accepted non-written guideline, the usage limit at this location has been set at 70% (consumption exceeding 70% significantly increases the likelihood of malfunction and reduces the mean time between failure (MTBF) and total cost of ownership (TCO)).

Thus, we have established the Marins of a region within which we might attempt to execute various performance enhancement approaches to achieve the best throughput. Numerous performance-enhancing approaches have been developed and put to use in practice over the years of WWW development and study (some of which are more difficult to apply than others).

The nature and complexity of the content that is available online have changed, and so have the performance-enhancing approaches (Sadre et al., 2008). During our preliminary investigation on this topic, we have identified more than 40 different strategies intended to improve the performance of multi-tier web application architecture.

KEYWORD

Distributed system is a system whose components are located on different networked computers, which communicate and coordinate their actions by passing messages to one another.

Some of them are no longer effective; others operate best with highly distributed systems; still, others only perform well under the most demanding workloads, where even 1 kB makes a difference, etc. We looked at 19 strategies in total in our analysis of the most popular techniques now in use that can be applied to the majority of WAs currently in use.

These strategies were examined using the following methodology: we identified each technique's goal and the means by which it attempts to achieve it, explained the implementation procedure, and provided an estimated time frame.

The tier of WA architecture that each approach affects is listed in order of preference. As anticipated, the fewest techniques affect the business logic tier of application architecture. Although an application's business logic can result in a bottleneck effect, fixing it is by far the most difficult and expensive task, and no enhancement technique can handle it.

If the application's business logic seems to be the bottleneck, this may indicate poor architecture choices or implementation. Code execution is not a particularly fruitful subsystem for performance improvement because it typically consumes between 5% and 15% of the entire response time (round trip).

According to Souders (2007), content delivery and query execution account for up to 80% of response time; as such, the majority of the investigated strategies aim to improve the efficiency of these subsystems. We chose six strategies with varying levels of complexity and implementation time for our research's experimental component.

The analysis consists of six properties:

- **Tier:** of the WA architecture affected by the technique.
- **Idea:** basic explanation of how the technique increases performance.
- **Implementation:** how is the technique implemented?
- **Time:** how long it took us (on average, if not otherwise specified) to use this technique in the three applications. Depending on the size and complexity of the application, various strategies' implementation times will differ (e.g., amount of code, number of servers).
- **Expected Results:** performance characteristics the technique affects.
- **Verification:** how is the performance gain measured?

Performance improvement calls for a full team of experts from all areas of WA development, from the front end (HTML, CSS, JavaScript) to the back end (database design, SQL queries, DBMS configuration, and administration), in order to plan and implement performance enhancement techniques and verify changes through benchmarking.

These teams must also assess the performance of the application architecture at each level because certain strategies could have undetected side effects that spread across the program and even result in a decline in performance at a different level. Some techniques call for the installation of extra server-side services.

When performing post-implementation stress testing, this must be taken into consideration because it complicates the application architecture and increases CPU and memory utilization (if additional services are operating on the same server).

General systems theory, which treats the application as a black box with a high rate of requests coming in and a high rate of responses leaving, can be a good place to start when looking to improve the performance of a WA. We determine which subsystems take the most time to produce responses when we break down the black box into its components.

If one subsystem consumes 80% of this time, we should aim to improve its performance rather than switching to another subsystem

KEYWORD

Performance improvement is measuring the output of a particular business process or procedure, then modifying the process or procedure to increase the output, increase efficiency, or increase the effectiveness of the process or procedure.

that uses only 5% of the time. When one subsystem's performance is improved, another one takes over as the main bottleneck. Defining quantitative parameters that specify the acceptable behavior of the system by benchmarking, detecting bottlenecks, adjusting, and re-benchmarking is an iterative process.

The performance measurement process includes creating quantifiable indicators that can be consistently followed for monitoring improvements in the achievement of service level objectives. With Was, the actual performance results frequently differ from what is desired or anticipated.

KEYWORD

Performance metrics are data used to track processes within a business. This is achieved using activities, employee behavior, and productivity as key metrics.

Performance metrics can consider factors including quality quantity, timeliness, and cost. Benchmarking and profiling are the two fundamental techniques for measuring performance. While benchmarking provides an answer to how well application functions, profiling provides an explanation for why the application performs as it does.

Since testing an application in a real-world setting is typically not practicable, we instead employ test versions or test cluster components and fake workloads. A crucial step in the performance benchmarking process is workload modeling.

In order to produce accurate measurements, the artificial workload must replicate a sample of the real workload, which would be actual users of the application. This can be achieved using various data sources, such as planned interactions, real-time user observations, and log file analysis.

Implementing the test workload needs to be as realistic as feasible to prevent the collection of inaccurate data and the making of poor conclusions.

8.3. WHAT CHARACTERIZES THE PERFORMANCE OF WEB APPLICATIONS?

Most "traditional" desktop program users are skilled at judging performance and know which tasks use a lot of resources and take longer to respond to. Many applications provide users with useful data that they can use to predict the processing time needed for a task or the amount of time left (e.g., progress bar when saving a file). Unfortunately, the majority of Web apps lack this transparency. Users are rarely informed about the reasons for the issue or offered meaningful support, despite the fact that the impact of poor performance is painfully perceived. Users cannot tell the difference between a link that directs them to a static HTTP page and a link that causes a dynamic page to be created, yet the response times can be significantly different.

If the page is already in the client cache, for example, the static link may not matter in terms of the server load, whereas creating a page from scratch would need resource-intensive database queries. Users typically are unable to determine whether or when they are leaving a Web application due to the hyperlink structure. All they will notice are changes in performance.

Each web application may perform below the established threshold values, but the extreme variability in the performance itself can leave users feeling confused, unhappy, and disillusioned with the program's usability. Additionally, it is difficult for users to manage a system's performance.

KEYWORD

Service provider is an organization that provides services, such as consulting, legal, real estate, communications, storage, and processing services, to other organizations.

Though users "cause the load," all they can do in the event of performance problems is to disconnect and try again later or use alternative services. Consequently, while improving system performance is important to solve this problem, users should be given better feedback.

Also, from the Web application developer's perspective, problems arise from factors beyond their control that can impact performance. The Internet, as a network between clients and servers in its current form offers no way to guarantee the quality of service.

A service provider can merely deploy sufficient bandwidth at the server or replicate servers, but they can't guarantee sufficient bandwidth all the way to the client. And developers have no influence on the performance of clients.

It is, therefore, important not only to test the functionality of Web applications on different platforms, but also to run performance tests over several network connections and client types (*see for example*, Williamson et al., 2002).

The methods known from "classic" performance analysis can also be used for Web applications, but the specific techniques and tools have to be adapted to the characteristics of Web applications (*see for example*, Casale, 2005).

The relevant methods will be discussed in the following sections. One of the most important aspects in this respect is the traffic and workload characterization (Crovella et al., 1998; Xia et al., 2005) because it is very difficult to predict user behavior and usage context due to the homogeneity and a large number of potential users.

And finally, the development of Web applications is short-lived, manifesting itself in short development cycles and comparatively long operation and maintenance phases. Many development processes don't integrate performance analyses for time and cost reasons, compensating for this shortcoming afterward by monitoring the system during normal operation.

KEYWORD

System performance is the amount of useful work done by a system - measured by the production speed of products of a predefined quality.

8.4. SYSTEM PERFORMANCE

Performance is one of the measurable quality attributes of a system which indicates the system's ability to meet its stakeholders' timing and capacity requirements (Bass, Clements, & Kazman, 2012).

According to Burkon (2013), performance dimensions include Response Time, Throughput, or Timeliness; and these dimensions are often expressed in terms of the time required to process a request, the number of requests per unit of time, or the ability to process a quantity of requests within a predetermined and acceptable time.

The importance of system performance cannot be overestimated due to its direct impact on what the end-users consider as acceptable time expectations and the capacity of the system. A recent study carried out by IDG Research (2013) on behalf of Ipanema Technologies indicated that 73% of enterprises surveyed cited poor application performance as the cause of a decrease in customer satisfaction and overall productivity.

In the same survey, 77% of respondents attributed great application performance to improved workforce productivity and 67% to improved customer satisfaction.

Perhaps of most concern in the study, 23% of respondents indicated that they would take their businesses elsewhere to put an end to the application performance frustration, and 9% of respondents say they will avoid working with the application remotely. This obviously has far-reaching implications on web applications, as they are mainly remote applications accessed via the web. The performance of a system can be impacted by several factors – including security overheads, inadequate computing resource capacity, bad application code, misconfigured infrastructure resources, and network related delays. This research work considers web application performance from three separate but related perspectives:

- Performance from the perspective of security impacts;
- Performance from the perspective of capacity planning, factoring in the influence of security mechanisms on performance and capacity planning; and
- Performance evaluation through analytical modeling to assist in predicting the performance of a given web application implementation, with security adequately factored in.

8.5. PERFORMANCE EVALUATION

Due to the quantitative nature of performance measures, they are widely considered to be the most objective set of parameters for measuring and quantifying the quality attributes of systems, particularly when considering acceptable system responsiveness or timeliness from the users' perspective (Figure 8.1).

Figure 8.1. *Performance evaluation.*

Performance evaluation can be achieved through two major traditional means – firstly, by the capturing of performance data from real-life performance monitoring and measurement, and secondly, via predictive techniques such as simulation and modeling.

Real-life performance measurement represents the system's actual operating conditions without exclusions or assumptions of any operational details. However, measurement techniques are found to be very expensive, time consuming, and intrusive of business activities, whereas predictive methods such as simulation and modeling are typically quicker and far less expensive, with analytical modeling being the quickest and the cheapest of these techniques (Pitts & Schormans, 2001).

8.5.1. Performance Measurement

Most research works in performance evaluation have centered on analytical modeling and simulation, mainly because of the predictive nature of the methods. One rarely comes across research works based purely on performance measurements; instead, most of the available studies on performance measurement tend to be studies where performance measurement has been used to validate the results of simulation studies or analytical models.

Remember

Extensive use of simulation methods has also been seen in computer network and communication research studies with the use of tools such as OPNET and OMNeT++ network modelers.

It is not uncommon to see performance measurement is used to validate the analyzes in simulation or analytical methods, as measurement provides the most reliable and accurate validation of analytical or simulation models and results (Eisenstadter, 1986).

A few studies (Kramer, 2011; Zaparanuks, 2009) have been conducted with a central focus on performance measurement. Kramer (2011) has studied the concept of Sustained System Performance in order to accurately assess system performance using estimation based on time-to-solution. Time-to-solution is basically a function of the time taken to complete a system task.

The measure is typically useful when comparing the performance of software applications in different computing environments (SAS Pub, 2009). Zaparanuks (2009) performed comparative experiments on a set of processors in order to evaluate the accuracy of three of the main testing infrastructures – perfctr, perfmon2, and PAPI.

While the arguments introduced by these studies are valid and could potentially steer improvements in the practice of performance measurement, they do not have any relevant contributions applicable to predictive performance evaluation methods and can only be applied to prototypes or real systems.

According to Haverkort (1998), performance measurement depends fundamentally on the availability of the real system.

8.5.2. Performance Metric Selection Issues

This will be done using experiments and performance measurements. The central issue in experiments and performance measurements is understanding the metric selection process.

If metrics are not selected objectively and structured, the likelihood of achieving accurate results could be greatly hampered. Literature and industry whitepapers abound with a huge number of potential metrics for performance evaluation for cloud, virtualized platforms, and web applications.

This situation presents the need for a systematic or scientific method of selecting evaluation metrics for specific purposes. According to Li et al. (2012), the evaluation of cloud services plays a role in the cost-benefit decisions relating to cloud adoption, and crucially, selecting suitable metrics is vital to evaluation implementations.

Li et al. argued that metric selection should be a foundation upon which benchmark selection should be based. Sadly, several cloud service evaluation studies in literature, be it performance evaluation, quality of service (QOS) evaluation, or security evaluation, have largely been carried out without proper scientific or systematic metric selection.

Although these studies focus mainly on cloud, these are easily adaptable to web application scenarios since most cloud applications are delivered as web applications and services.

KEYWORD

Quality of service (QoS) is the use of mechanisms or technologies that work on a network to control traffic and ensure the performance of critical applications with limited network capacity.

8.5.3. Metric Selection Process

According to Li et al. (2013), the first stage in cloud evaluation methodology is to state a clear purpose for which the service evaluation is required and to identify which services and features require evaluation. An evaluation aims to understand the effect of security measures on the performance of web applications hosted on a virtualized platform. This forms the starting point for the metric selection flow process.

8.5.4. Performance Benchmarks

Benchmark is another concept worthy of mentioning in any performance measurement discussion. Benchmarks are standard programs developed for the purpose of system performance evaluation. These programs or loads are run on systems to capture performance data resulting from their execution.

According to Lee et al. (2013), cloud machines' performance evaluation benchmarks should cover a typical VM's components, such as CPU speed, disk I/O, memory, and network I/O. Proper selection of benchmarks is vital to achieving representative results in performance testing; unfortunately, this is an area in which many studies in the literature have fallen short.

Did you Know?

According to Burkon (2013), performance dimensions include response time, throughput or timeliness; and these dimensions are often expressed in terms of time required to process a request, the number of requests per unit of time or the ability to process a quantity of requests within a predetermined and acceptable time.

8.6. CHARACTERIZING THE WORKLOAD

Selecting an appropriate workload is decisive for a performance evaluation study to be successful and supply meaningful results. Only a representative workload model can help to make representative statements about a system's performance behavior.

When selecting the workload model, we have to consider two dimensions. The first differentiation concerns the excitability of the workload model, i.e., when measuring techniques should be used for performance evaluation or the non-excitability of techniques that model applications.

The second differentiation concerns the restriction to the actual workload (that is executable by definition) or the use of an artificial workload, which is generated by load generators rather than by real users.

The use of a real workload is actually less significant for performance prediction. Though we could study the system under real load, i.e., in real-time operation, measuring it would only show us a posteriori whether and when performance problems have occurred.

Extracting characteristics yielded from studying the real load (*see* Williamson et al., 2005) and combining typical elements of the real workload (e.g., selecting typical requests), and so-called synthetic workload in experiments are more useful methods.

Synthetic workload means that requests identical to those occurring in the real world are used but with an artificially created frequency and sequence. For example, it is possible to study how the system would behave under a changed workload (i.e., the same types of requests but with different arrival rates).

Stress tests also require the creation of a synthetic workload model. If we do entirely without the kind of components that typically occur in the real workload, we speak of artificial workload models. Executable artificial workload models could consist of requests used to knowingly try to represent "meaningless" user input, for example, to find security flaws in a system.

The class of non-executable workload models is another artificial workload model; in this case, we would have to find a suitable abstraction level in the modeling effort. A model used in the analysis of queuing networks describes the workload by the frequency in which requests arrive at the system (e.g., as a stochastic process) and the expected consumption of resources, the so-called service demand (D), measured in the time units a request needs to have a system component processed.

The workload cannot be meaningfully described by one single type of request, nor is it meant to model it as an average value from the set of all requests, especially for complex Web applications. Such a single-class workload model is easy to handle (with regard to both its modeling and measurements) and can be used for initial estimates of a system's performance.

In addition, we need a differentiated description of the workload to yield specific findings on the system performance behavior. This means that we have to use a multi-class workload model. The basic idea of multi-class workload models is to group similar requests into a loaded class and then describe all requests occurring within a load class by a representative from that class.

This approach uses clustering methods that recognize similarities in requests and determine representative load parameters. Clustering first defines the workload characteristics by which the similarity should be investigated (for example, this can be the arrival frequency or the service demanded from specific resources).

The clustering principle is particularly easy to visualize when two parameters are used, but the method can also be used for an arbitrary number of parameters (which may have to be transformed before the analysis and should be studied as to mutual independence).

The heterogeneity of documents and their multimodality require a detailed description of the workload. Only in a simplistic model can an HTTP request be seen as a unit of the workload; a performance analysis requires classification and representation of

KEYWORD

Workload is the amount of computing resources and time it takes to complete a task or generate an outcome.

a wide range of requests. The field of workload characterization can be even more difficult because user behavior is often hard to predict and changes continually. To solve these problems, we could use generative or learning models for workload characterization (*see* Haring et al., 2001).

8.7. PERFORMANCE OPTIMIZATION METHODS

Measures to improve the performance of Web applications are primarily targeted at shortening response times or increasing throughput. However, these goals can be achieved only if we identify and remove a system's bottleneck (or bottlenecks).

KEYWORD

Bottleneck is a point of congestion in a production system (such as an assembly line or a computer network) that stops or severely slows the system.

We call the component with the highest utilization the primary bottleneck, which also primarily requires performance-improving measures. A bottleneck can basically be removed by reducing the load on the bottleneck component (e.g., reducing the transmitted file sizes to remove load from the network) or increasing the component's performance (e.g., increasing the bandwidth of the network connection).

Once we have removed the primary bottleneck, we typically observe that another component will become a bottleneck, known as the secondary bottleneck. From the performance perspective, an optimal system is a balanced system in which the utilization of all system components is (approximately) equal, so there will be no primary bottleneck.

An optimal strategy to improve performance should, therefore, not only look at one single component but consider the system as a whole. In principle, any system component can represent a bottleneck, and performance problems in practice are frequently due to delays in the transmission network (Internet) and server-side delays due to dynamically generated pages (e.g., high startup times of CGI scripts and time-intensive database queries).

The subsections discuss selected performance optimization methods (*see* Tracy et al., 1997; Killeen, 2002 for a detailed description).

8.7.1. Acceleration Within a Web Application

The first class of methods applies to the Web application itself, which means that it must be considered in the application development process. This class includes, by definition, all methods that aim at shortening the execution time of the application on the server, but also adaptations within the Web application that shorten the communication time with the client or lead to shorter execution time on the client.

The following methods are examples of this class:

- **Load Balancing between Client and Server:** An important question for the design of Web applications is the load distribution between client and server. More specifically, we have to decide how much of the application logic should be processed by the client and how much at the server. For example, the client could check data input in forms. These controls are relevant both for security reasons and performance reasons.
- **Embedding Server-Side Applications:** Web servers offer a CGI (Common Gateway Interface) that can be used to forward HTTP requests to other programs in the server for further processing. From the performance perspective, we could investigate alternative embedding possibilities, e.g., by using servlets.
- **Pre-Generating Web Content:** The dynamic generation of pages based on information from other applications (typically databases) is a computing-intensive and time-consuming process. It would, therefore, be a good idea to pre-generate popular pages and then make them available as static pages at the cost of their to-the-second accuracy (Sidon, 1998; Schrefl et al., 2003).
- **Adapting an HTTP Response to the Client's Capabilities:** Though web application developers normally have no influence on the options site visitors configure in their clients (e.g., disabling the automatic download of images), they have to take these options into account in the application development process.

Web applications can poll many client settings (e.g., JavaScript) to present more personalized information to visitors.

This allows for increasing the QOS subjectively perceived by the users, in particular when embedding multimedia content; we should take the capabilities of clients into account to ensure, for instance, that both the server and the network won't get overloaded by transmitting large data sets, which wouldn't be displayed correctly in the client anyway.

KEYWORD

CGI (Common gateway interface) is the middleware in which the web servers execute the user request from an external program.

Compromises in the representation quality of multimedia content can be meaningful in favor of improved performance.

Remember

According to Haverkort (1998) the performance measurement depends fundamentally on the availability of the real system.

8.7.2. Reducing Transmission Time

The network often represents the bottleneck for web applications in which the clients and servers are connected over a WAN. Future Internet protocols will support more options to negotiate the QOS between clients and servers. The two approaches briefly described in the subsections have been used successfully with the current technological state-of-the-art.

8.7.2.1. Web Caching and Content Pre-Fetching

Many Web browsers store frequently requested pages on the client's local hard disk (or in the main memory). When the client visits such a page again, it fetches the page from its cache rather than forwarding the request to the server.

A continuation of this concept is Web proxy servers, which assume the same function as caches on the Internet, i.e., they serve replies to client requests from their cache rather than from the server. In addition to reducing the transmission delay, Web caching removes load from the Web server. Web content pre-fetching is based on the same idea, but it additionally tries to predict the pages a user will access next by loading these pages proactively into the cache memory. The strategy of determining which pages should be held in the cache and for how long is important both in Web caching and content pre-fetching. Recent approaches try to apply methods from AI and machine learning (Park et al., 2005). To make the right decision, we have to weigh the cache capacity, the access time, and actuality (Labrinidis & Roussopoulos, 2004; Podlipnig & Boszormenyi, 2003). A poorly configured proxy or cache server can even cause response times to increase. From a protocol point of view, the W3C has issued an RFC on caching in HTTP. A well-known and commonly used caching tool is for example SQUID.

8.7.2.2. Web Server Replication and Load Balancing

Web server replication is another technique that does not forward a client request directly to the addressed server but redirects it to a replicate of that server. In addition to shortening the transmission time, this technique removes some server load.

A simple way of implementing this technique is so-called mirror sites, offered explicitly as alternative servers to users. The drawback is that users normally don't know what server offers the best performance, and the site operator has no control over load balancing. These problems can be avoided by using implicit mirroring.

KEYWORD

Load balancing is the method of distributing network traffic equally across a pool of resources that support an application.

Externally, implicit mirroring lets users access only one logical address (URL) of a server while the request is then internally forwarded to a replicate of that server. Another benefit of implicit mirroring is that the users always need to know only one single address, and the server replica can be easily added or removed without informing users of changes in the address.

Surrogate servers represent a technique that combines caching and replication. A Web server forwards requests to a surrogate server. The surrogate server tries to reply to the request from its cache and accesses the original Web server in the event of a cache miss.

Surrogate servers can also be used jointly by several Web servers. A network composed of surrogate servers is also known as a content delivery network (CDN; Gadde et al., 2000).

8.7.3. Server Tuning

The last class of methods is aimed at improving the execution platform of a Web application. This group includes primarily hardware upgrades (main memory expansion, CPU acceleration, faster disks) and optimized settings in the Web server (e.g., disabling the DNS lookup for log files).

We refer our readers to the manual of their preferred Web server and relevant information and discussion forums on the Internet.

8.8. ANALYTICAL TECHNIQUES (FIGURE 8.2)

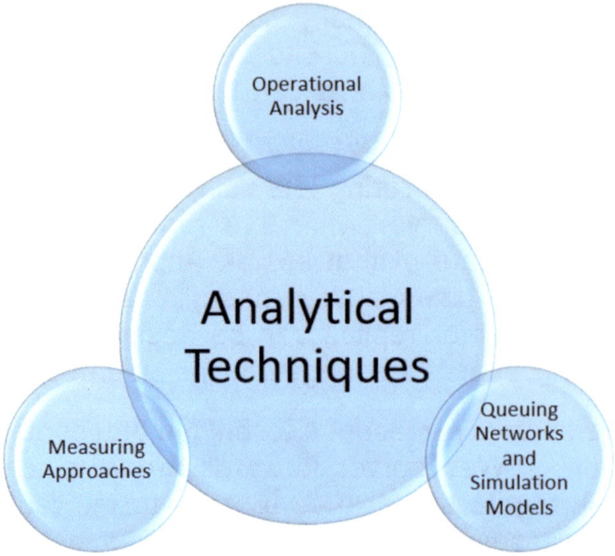

Figure 8.2. *Analytical techniques.*

8.8.1. Operational Analysis

An operational analysis takes some basic measurable (operational) quantities, primarily the number of completed requests (C) within a defined observation period, T, to look at the components of a system for analytical purposes. Referring to a system component as 'k,' we can define the station k's throughput as $X_k = C_k/T$.

If we introduce a quantity B_k, to specify the time during which the station was busy processing requests, then we can determine the service time for a request at station k as $s_k = B_k/C_k$. The demand D for a service in a request to a station puts the service time in relation to the total number of completed requests: $D_k = s_k \times C_k/C = B_k/C$. Similarly, we can write $X_k = X \times C_k/C$ to define a relationship between the system throughput, X, and the throughput per component, X_k.

The utilization U of a station is defined as the time during which the station is busy, i.e., $U_k = B_k/T = (B_k/T) \times (C_k/C_k) = (B_k/C_k) \times (C_k/T) = X_k \times s_k = X \times D_k$. This relationship is known as the utilization law. The utilization law can be used even in the early phases of a Web application development project for rough performance estimates.

Example: Let's look at a Web server consisting of one CPU and two disks. Measurements have observed the system for an hour. A total of 7,200 requests have been completed during this period. The utilization was as follows: CPU = 10%; disk 1 = 30%; disk 2 = 40%. We can use this information to determine the service demand per component as follows:

X = C/T = 7200/3600 requests per second = 2 requests per second

DCPU = UCPU/X = 0.1/2 sec = 50 msec

Ddisk1 = Udisk1/X = 0.3/2 sec = 150 msec

Ddisk2 = Udisk2/X = 0.4/2 sec = 200 msec

Little's Law (1961) defines a relationship between response time, throughput, and the number of requests in the system (N).

If a request spends R time units on average in the system, and if X requests per time unit are completed on average, then an average of N = R * X requests must be spent time in the system. Example: Let's assume that the mean response time of all 7,200 requests from the above example was found to be 0.9 seconds.

Consequently, an average of N = R * X = 0.9 * 2 = 1.8 requests spent time in the Web server during the observation period. Little's Law can also be applied to a single station and is then defined as $N_k = R_k \times X_k$.

In addition to the fundamental laws that can be used to derive performance quantities from measured data, an operational analysis also offers a way to analyze bottlenecks. A bottleneck is a station that first reaches 100% utilization as the load increases.

We can see from the utilization law $U_k = X \times D_k$ that this is the station with the largest service demand. We can also derive an upper limit for the system throughput from this: $X < 1/D_k$. An upper limit can normally not be defined for the response time, but we can define a lower limit out of the consideration that a request spends at least D_k time units in each station, so that $R>E_kDk$.

The analysis becomes more complex if we introduce different classes of requests. We would then have to consider $C_{c,k}$, namely the completed requests per class c and station k. We will not describe all operational laws for multi-classes in detail because corresponding formulas and application examples can be found in the literature (Jain, 1991; Menasce & Almeida, 2002).

KEYWORD

Operational analysis compares current business performance with historical data to review business operations.

8.8.2. Queuing Networks and Simulation Models

Queuing networks represent a modeling technique for all systems characterized by a set of components that send requests (called sources) and a set of components that process requests (called stations, as we know from the above discussion).

A source sends requests of type c with a rate of λ_c to a network of stations. In contrast to operational analysis, queuing networks look at requests processed in a station more closely, distinguishing between a waiting area (and a related waiting time, W_i) and the actual service area (with service time s_i).

KEYWORD

Queuing Networks are models where customers (service requests) arrive at service stations (servers) to be served.

The arrival and processing of requests are described by stochastic processes (Jain, 1991), i.e., by specifying the distribution of arrival times and service times per station. We can now prepare a state transition chart for a single station, where the number of requests in the queue or service area defines a state.

State transitions are defined by the arrival times and service times, respectively, by arrival and service rates. We can now validate such a system with respect to the existence of a stationary distribution to determine probabilities for the number of requests in the queue and in the service area.

We then take these probabilities to calculate expected values for the performance quantities. It should be noted that solving these systems analytically for arbitrary distributions is impossible. Instead, we would use discrete event simulation to solve cases that cannot be solved analytically (Jain, 1991).

If we look at how several such service stations interact, each station in so-called separable networks can be seen in isolation and analyzed by calculating the stationary distribution. A separable network is a network in which a station's branching probabilities and service times do not depend on the distribution of requests over other stations.

This means that we can calculate static visit ratios and arrival rates per station. Alternatively, we can prepare a state transition chart for the entire system, where a vector with the number of requests at each service station describes a state.

This solution technique is known as convolution; the complexity of the calculation increases exponentially with the number of requests and stations. Both the solution using separable networks and the one using convolution determine probabilities for the distribution of requests across the components and derive additional performance quantities from it.

An alternative to calculating the stationary distribution is the mean value analysis (MVA). The MVA takes the arrival rates per class, λ_c, and the service demands per class and station, $D_{c,k}$, as input parameters. As the name implies, this technique calculates mean values (or expected values) directly from the performance quantities.

We refer our readers to Menasce & Almeida (2002) for a detailed discussion of the modeling power of queuing networks for Web applications. All analytical techniques introduced so far are based on the assumption of an open system, at which requests arrive from one (infinite) source.

If the total number of requests that can be made to a system is limited, as is the case, for instance, in batch processing systems, then other laws, relationships, and solution techniques apply. However, since we would typically model Web applications as open systems, we will not discuss analytical techniques for closed systems.

KEYWORD

System behavior is described as continuous when it behaves predictably through its range of states.

In summary, we can say that analytical techniques are well suited for an initial estimate of a Web application's performance in the early development phases. Measurements can determine the workload parameters required for analysis, but we could also use best-case and worst-case assumptions to obtain an estimate of the system behavior in extreme situations.

The major benefits of this analysis are its relatively simple use and the fact that the system does not necessarily have to exist yet.

8.8.3. Measuring Approaches

A measuring approach instruments an existing system (either the real system in normal operation or a test system). To this end, measuring approaches use timers to measure the time at well-defined system points or use counters to count the occurrence of certain events, and the basic data they collect can be used to deduce performance quantities.

Such instrumentation in software is often enhanced and supported by special measuring hardware (particularly in the network area). Performance measurement methods (Faulkner Information

Services, 2001) have an inherent risk of falsifying the system behavior by the measurement itself.

A falsification of the system behavior (intrusion) by measuring software can hardly be avoided. Some approaches are being investigated to see whether measurement and simulation could be linked so that a "virtual time" could be captured during measuring experiments, which could then be used to determine performance quantities.

Other approaches try to estimate the intrusion rate to then determine corresponding confidence intervals for the performance quantities. Another approach to reducing falsification uses hardware monitors, i.e., the system's own hardware, to evaluate the system under test. This means that this approach hardly uses the resources of the system under test for monitoring purposes.

TIPS

The clustering principle is particularly easy to visualize when two parameters are used, but the method can also be used for an arbitrary number of parameters.

Load-generating tools have become very important in measurement practice. Load generators generate synthetic or artificial workloads, allowing the analyst to study the system behavior under a hypothetical workload.

A load generator can be either a self-written program or script that sends HTTP requests to a server and determines the response time from the difference in time stamps captured in the client rather than interpreting the response to visualize it in a Web browser.

Special forms of measuring tools are so-called benchmarks. A benchmark is an artificial workload model that serves to compare systems. To use a benchmark, the system has to process a defined set of requests, and the system's performance during this process is then typically expressed in one single metric.

While some benchmarks have become popular in other fields to compare system performance (e.g., the Linpack benchmark to calculate the fastest supercomputer of the world; see http://www.top500.org), benchmarks that especially test the performance of Web applications and their execution platforms are still in their infancy.

One example is the Spec Web benchmark (see http://www.spec.org), which specifies a standardized workload consisting of a set of static and dynamic requests.

SUMMARY

1. **Performance of Web Application:** This chapter summarizes about the performance of web applications. What characterizes the performance of web applications? Also, it explains the system definition and indicators and system performance.
2. Performance Evaluation has also been discussed under this: performance Measurement, Performance metric selection issues, Metric Selection process, and Performance Benchmarks.
3. **System Definition and Indicators:** This part of the chapter explains the system definition and indicators in detail. Simulation and characterizing the Workload have also been explained.
4. **Analytical Techniques:** The end of the chapter explains the different analytical techniques, such as – operational analysis, queuing networks and simulation models, and measuring approaches.

Performance optimization methods such as – acceleration within a web application, reducing transmission time, and server tuning have been briefly explained under this.

REVIEW QUESTIONS

1. What do you understand by the performance of web applications?
2. What characterizes the performance of web applications?
3. What is system definition and indicators?
4. What do you understand by system performance?
5. Explain performance evaluation?
6. What do you understand by measuring approaches?
7. Explain performance optimization methods?
8. Explain the different analytical techniques?

MULTIPLE CHOICE QUESTIONS

1. Performance testing is used to uncover ____________ problems.

a. Performance
b. Validation
c. Verification
d. None of the above

2. **Amongst which of the following is/are the performance testing objectives?**
   a. At what point does performance become unacceptable
   b. System components are responsible for performance degradation
   c. Average response time for users under a variety of loading conditions
   d. All of the above
3. **What is the first step in the software development lifecycle?**
   a. System design
   b. Coding
   c. System testing
   d. Preliminary investigation and analysis
4. **Model selection is based on _________**
   a. Requirements
   b. Development team and users
   c. Project type and associated risk
   d. All of the above
5. **Which of the following activities is not recommended for software processes in software engineering?**
   a. Software evolution
   b. Software verification
   c. Software testing and validation
   d. Software designing

Answers to Multiple Choice Questions

1. (a) 2. (d) 3. (d) 4. (d) 5. (b)

REFERENCES

1. Babatunde, J., (2015). *Evaluating the Impact of Security Measures on Performance of Secure Web Applications Hosted on Virtualized Platforms.* repository.uel.ac.uk. University of East London for the degree of Professional Doctorate in Information Security. Available at: https://repository.uel.ac.uk/download/860cd9c0802ea8ba5d31f5df91e3bdbfb919eee114bac2e69ee2a03f9cb7612f/20753811/John%20Babatunde.pdf (accessed on 04 March 2023).
2. Cassone, G., et al., (n.d). *Web Performance Testing and Measurement: A Complete Approach.* www.agileconnection.com. TILAB. Available at: https://www.agileconnection.com/sites/default/files/article/file/2012/XDD3579filelistfilename1_0.pdf (accessed on 04 March 2023).

3. Jensen, O., (2008). *The Performance of Web Applications*. info.headspin.io. Aberdeen Group. Available at: https://info.headspin.io/hubfs/Analyst%20Reports/5136-RR-performance-web-application.pdf (accessed on 04 March 2023).
4. Jugo, I., Kermek, D., & Meštrović, A., (2014). Analysis and evaluation of web application performance enhancement techniques. *Lecture Notes in Computer Science*, 40–56. Available at: https://doi.org/10.1007/978-3-319-08245-5_3.
5. Marang, A. Z., (2018). *Analysis of Web Performance Optimization and Its Impact on User Experience.* kth.diva-portal.org. KTH Royal Institute of Technology. Available at: https://kth.diva-portal.org/smash/get/diva2:1228341/FULLTEXT01.pdf (accessed on 04 March 2023).
6. Singh, J., (2014). *Performance Analysis of Web Applications*. Academia.edu. Academia. Available at: https://www.academia.edu/4300420/Performance_analysis_of_web_Applications (accessed on 04 March 2023).
7. Zhou, Q., Ye, H., & Ding, Z., (2012). Performance analysis of web applications based on user navigation. *Physics Procedia, 24*, 1319–1328. Available at: https://doi.org/10.1016/j.phpro.2012.02.197.

INDEX

J

K

L

M

T

Printed in the United States
by Baker & Taylor Publisher Services